Edward Herbert Maxwell

Griffin ahoy!

A yacht cruise to the Levant and wanderings in Egypt, Syria, the Holy Land, Greece and Italy in 1881

Edward Herbert Maxwell

Griffin ahoy!
A yacht cruise to the Levant and wanderings in Egypt, Syria, the Holy Land, Greece and Italy in 1881

ISBN/EAN: 9783337197322

Printed in Europe, USA, Canada, Australia, Japan

Cover: Foto ©ninafisch / pixelio.de

More available books at **www.hansebooks.com**

GRIFFIN AHOY!

A YACHT CRUISE TO THE LEVANT,

AND

WANDERINGS IN EGYPT, SYRIA, THE HOLY LAND, GREECE, AND ITALY, IN 1881.

ATHENS.

GRIFFIN AHOY!

A YACHT CRUISE TO THE LEVANT,

AND

WANDERINGS IN EGYPT, SYRIA, THE HOLY LAND
GREECE AND ITALY IN 1881.

BY

GENERAL E. H. MAXWELL, C.B.

IN ONE VOLUME.

LONDON
HURST AND BLACKETT, PUBLISHERS
13, GREAT MARLBOROUGH STREET
1882

Dedicated

to

JOHN BAIRD, ESQ.

OF KNOYDART,

IN REMEMBRANCE OF **MANY HAPPY** HOURS

ON BOARD **THE** "GRIFFIN."

CONTENTS.

CHAPTER I.

ON BOARD THE "GRIFFIN."

The "Griffin" and her Crew—Kidby, the Steward—Arrangement of our Time—Our First Night on Board—The Bay of Biscay—The Channel Fleet—The "Griffin" in a Gale—Sheltered by the Berlengers—Gibraltar—Changes in the Army—Disappearance of Esprit de Corps—Visit to Algesiras—The Arena for Bull-fights—Malaga—Oran—Algiers—Amusing Mistake—Arab Quarter 3

CHAPTER II.

PROGRESS OF OUR CRUISE.

Malta—Old Reminiscences—The New Forest—Story of a Bear—Burmola—The Inquisitors' Palace—A Strong Gale—A Peculiarity of the Mediterranean—Our Cook—A Fine Morning at Sea—Anchored off Cyprus—Quaint Tradition—Chapel of St. Lazarus—Ancient English Tombs—Land-birds at Sea—H.M.S. "Coquette"—Tradition of Omah—Alexandretta—A Sporting-party—A Stormy Day 25

CONTENTS.

CHAPTER III.

IN EASTERN CLIMES.

Walk to La Fontaine—Alexandretta—The Ship of the Desert—
Madame Cottoni's Soirée Dansante—Gun Practice in Beyas
Bay—A Pilgrimage to Antioch—The Beilan Pass—Country
frequented by Brigands—The Syrian Gates—Hospitably
entertained by a Jew—Antioch—The Church of St. John—
Public Baths—Palace built by Antiochus—Grateful old
Lady 47

CHAPTER IV.

EASTERN EXPERIENCES.

Visit of Mr. Martin, the Missionary—The Bazaar at Antioch—
Journey to the Groves of Daphne—A Grotto and Cascade—
The Orontes—Mr. Essom, the Missionary—Our Jewish Host
and his Family—Legend of the Lake—Ascent of the Defiles of
Amanus—The Syrian Gates—The Beilan Pass—A Sporting-
party—A Picnic to Beilan—Accident to Parker—Quarantine
at Alexandria—Process of Fumigation . . . 67

CHAPTER V.

THE PYRAMIDS.

Cairo—Shepherd's Hotel—Eastern Scenes—Cairo becoming Galli-
cised—View from the Platform of the Citadel—Heliopolis—
Ancient Obelisk—Ostrich Farm—The Virgin's Tree—The Mu-
seum—The Nile—Road to the Pyramids—The Pyramids—
Temple of the Sphinx—Exploration of a Pyramid—Village of
Geezeh—Egyptian Soldiers 89

CHAPTER VI.

EGYPTIAN ANTIQUITIES.

The Island of Roda—The Nilometer—Palace of Ibrahim Pasha—

Old Cairo, or Babylon—Mosque of Amer—Tent Colours—
Snipe-shooting—Loading Egyptian Donkeys—The Pyramids of
Sakkarah—Exploration of the Serapeum—The Tomb of Ti—
Employment of Idle Hours—The Baths of Heliopolis—Archæo-
logical Discoveries 111

CHAPTER VII.

VISIT TO THE HOLY LAND.

A Journey to Syria—Proposed Mode of Travelling—The Commo-
dore's Camp—Dispersion of our Party—Anchored off Jaffa, or
Joppa—An old Sailor—Howard's Hotel—Ibrahim Dehrony,
our Dragoman—Parting Look at the "Griffin"—Oranges of
Joppa—Scripture Localities—Ramleh—Tomb of the Maccabees
—Latron—In Jerusalem at last 129

CHAPTER VIII.

IN JERUSALEM.

The Streets of Jerusalem—Pictures—St. Stephen's Gate—Gethse-
mane—Traditions and Prophecies relating to Jerusalem—
David's Tower—A Celebrated Hebrew Scholar—Phylacteries—
An American Party—The Mount of Olives—Hospital of St.
John—Church of the Sepulchre—Tombs of the Kings and of
the Judges—Valley of Jehoshaphat—Church of the Ascension—
Tomb of David 147

CHAPTER IX.

SCENES IN THE HOLY LAND.

Pilgrimage to Jericho—Captain Ossum and the "Griffin"—The
Tomb of Absalom—Bethany—Wilderness of Judæa—A Painful
Sight—Plains of Jordan and the Dead Sea—We meet again
our American Friends—Women from a Bedouin Camp—Jericho
—Banks of the Jordan—Story of a Sportsman—The Tomb of
Moses—Convent of Marsaba—We Part with our Escort—An
old Story—Bethlehem—Traditions 165

CHAPTER X.

THE JEWS IN SYRIA.

Mosque on the Site of the Temple—The Mosque of Aksa—Fountain in the Court—The Cradle of Jesus—Descent of the Holy Fire—Departure from Jerusalem—A Self-willed old Lady—The Russian Hospice—Pilgrims—Jews—The Jews' Wailing-place—Smoking in the East—In the "Griffin" again—Departure from Joppa—St. Jean d'Acre—Anchored off Haifa . . . 191

CHAPTER XI.

IN THE FOOTSTEPS OF CHRIST.

Preparations for our Start—Ibrahim indignant—Our Steeds and their Riders—Expedition to Nazareth and the Sea of Galilee—Mount Carmel—Appearance of the Country—The River Kishon—Destruction of Trees in Syria—The Plains of Esdraelon—Ploughing Operations—Nazareth—The Latin Convent—Brother John of Nazareth—Visits to various Memorials of Christ—Mount Tabor—Sea of Galilee—Tiberias—Ibrahim's Wound 213

CHAPTER XII.

THE LEBANON AND ANTI-LEBANON.

St. Jean d'Acre—Cross-grained Turks—The Tyrian Ladder—Tyre—Prophecies Confirmed—Sidon—Beyrout—Lady Hester Stanhope—Eccentric Coachmen—We Part with Ibrahim—Ibrahim Dehrony—Tradition of St. George—The Oriental Hotel—Start for Damascus—Ascent of Lebanon—Chalcis—Valley of Wady-el-Kurn—The River Abana—The Anti-Lebanon—Approach to Damascus 243

CHAPTER XIII.

DAMASCUS.

Damascus compared with Constantinople—Our Hotel—Horse Fair—

CONTENTS.

Bazaars of the Different Trades—The Brass Bazaar—The Grand Mosque—The Street called Straight—Prostrate Columns—House of Ananias—The Gate Bab-el-Jabyeh—Scene of Paul's Conversion—Persecution of Christians—Grave of Buckle the Historian—Houses of the Wealthy Inhabitants—The Public Gardens—Circassian Refugees—Drive along the Banks of the Abana—Arrival at Beyrout 259

CHAPTER XIV.

GREECE RE-VISITED.

Our Pilgrimage Accomplished—Views of various Islands—The Isles of Greece—Athens—The Piræus—The Massacre of English Gentlemen—A Russian Friend—Trains between the Piræus and Athens—Athenian Cabs—Change in the Aspect of Athens—Remains of Antiquity—Discovery of an Ancient Cemetery—The Tomb of Agamemnon—The Excavations of Dr Schliemann 285

CHAPTER XV.

FAREWELL TO THE "GRIFFIN."

Departure from Athens—Notes of our Voyage—Stromboli—Story of a Letter—Naples again—Sail to Ischia—View of Sorrento—A Grim old Building—Terrible Discovery—A Wearisome Ascent—A Perfectly-situated Hotel—Reminiscences of an Earthquake—A Sad Story—Beauties of Ischia—Monte Nuovo—The Commodore and Princess Serenaded—Termination of our Cruise—The Czar's Yacht—A Few Hours in Naples—The Aquarium 307

CHAPTER I.

ON BOARD THE "GRIFFIN."

THE "GRIFFIN" AND HER CREW—HENRY, THE STEWARD—ARRANGEMENT OF OUR TIME—OUR FIRST NIGHT ON BOARD—THE DAY OF DEPART—THE CHANNEL FLEET—THE "GRIFFIN" IN A GALE—SPELT OUT BY THE TELEGRAPH—GIBRALTAR—CHANGES IN THE ARMY—DISAPPEARANCE OF ESPRIT DE CORPS—VISIT TO ALGECIRAS—THE ARENA FOR BULL-FIGHTS—MALAGA—ORAN—ALGIERS—AMUSING MISTAKE—ARAB QUARTERS.

CHAPTER I.

THE sun shone brightly on the snow-covered ground as we left our comfortable home to proceed on our travels. We had been invited to accompany our kind friends of Knoydart, in their yacht the *Griffin*, on a cruise to the Mediterranean, and the hope of basking in sunshine on the calm blue sea made us accept with pleasure this welcome invitation.

I will pass over our long journey from the north to Falmouth. The train dashed along through a snow-covered country; sometimes the white mantle was deeper at one place than at another, but the whole of Scotland and England was lying under a virgin pall, and the cold was intense.

On the morning of the 19th of January, 1881, we all assembled at breakfast in the Falmouth Hotel. Our host will appear in these pages as the Commodore, our gentle hostess as the Princess. Then there were Miss Hare, and Susan, Kildonan, and Parker, my wife and self; all told, a party of eight.

The snowstorms everywhere were very severe about this time, and the papers were full of disasters by sea and land.

On the 22nd of January we embarked on board the *Griffin*. The shades of evening were closing around, and intense frost was in the air. We bade farewell to England, and we could but wonder what our fate would be as we steamed out of Falmouth Harbour, and big waves beat against us and made us all tumble about, for we had not yet got our sea-legs.

The *Griffin* is a fine, barque-rigged yacht of three hundred and fifteen tons, with auxiliary screw. She is built as strong as a gunboat, and is very fast. Often we have gone by the log thirteen knots. She has a deck saloon, and immediately facing the door of this cabin are the stairs leading down to where the sleeping-berths are, as well as to dining-saloon, pantry, &c. The ladies' cabins are divided from the gentlemen's by a wooden partition which extends along the centre of the vessel, and on each side is a sea-water bath. My cabin was most luxurious, and was next to my wife's, from which it was separated by a curtain.

The crew consisted of Captain Oman, first and second mate, and seven able-bodied seamen, as fine a set of fellows as you could meet anywhere. The engineer had three men under him in his department, one cook and cook's mate, one steward and two under-stewards. There were also the Princess's maid and her sister. Besides all these belonging to the yacht, was worthy M'Gregor, Kildonan's gamekeeper, whose bagpipes were often heard on the wide Atlantic Ocean.

"Kidby" the steward was a most attentive man, most civil on all occasions, and always ready with any restorative. He had a slight impediment in his speech, which rather imparted zest to his remarks.

Our day began generally about half-past seven a.m., when a knock at my cabin-door was followed by the announcement that the bath was ready. A plunge into the salt water was very refreshing. This was followed by a cup of tea. Breakfast was at nine, luncheon at two, and dinner at seven. In the evening dominoes, chess, and literature, combined with cigars and cigarettes, made the time pass pleasantly; but I must own that in rough weather chess was impossible, and dominoes sometimes not very practicable.

The sea was very rough during our first night on board. The waves curled up like wild demons against the round port in my cabin, which was firmly fixed, and then retired, seemingly baffled, to bang against the vessel's sides, and leap frantically on to the deck and rush madly back into the sea. Hour after hour passed, and this maniac dance continued; yet in the morning when we got on deck, instead of meeting gloomy faces, we were told that we had made a splendid run during the night. As the day went on, strange, oil-skinned figures, whom it was difficult to recognise except by their voices, appeared staggering about in solemn pomposity.

This first day was Sunday. The Commodore read prayers in presence of the men off duty and as many of our party as could face the ordeal of remaining in the cabin. We rolled and tumbled through the Bay of Biscay till Monday night.

On Tuesday we were glad to learn that we had left the bay, and were no less pleased to hail the beautiful morning which greeted our appearance on deck. The Channel Fleet were exercising on our port bow, and a school of porpoises gambolled and played before our ship. We were all in great spirits, now that the dreaded bay was passed, and we were near the coast of sunny Portugal. All storms were over, but the wind blew in gusts from the south-west, dead against us. The sea got up, the breeze freshened. At length a gale came on, and we were exposed to all the fury of a sou'-wester right in our teeth. The *Griffin* behaved nobly. Sometimes she dashed her head against a huge wave, and the sea leaped over her bows and swept along the decks. But, apparently revived by her plunge, she rose over the next wave and shook herself free from the effects of the former attack. The wind moaned in the rigging, and wave after wave succeeded each other; sometimes a great fierce one, followed occasionally by a tremendous roll of green water. As we looked around, the whole ocean appeared as a series of dark caverns, from which the spray flew like smoke from a gun, and the heavens were gloomy and lowering above us. The gale was so violent that we were unable to proceed, but hove to, and so passed the night. Wednesday morning broke dull and stormy. The wind was still blowing a strong gale from the south-west. We were near the Berlengers, lonely, barren rocks on which is a lighthouse. The sea dashed against them, mounting high up into the air and breaking into cascades of snow-white spray.

The Commodore thought, if we could get to leeward of these rocks, we might have a comparatively quiet time for dinner. The attempt accordingly was made, and, having changed our course, we had the wind on our beam for a short time, and staggered towards the slight protection these rocks afforded. The shelter was very small, still it was a change, and we all appeared at dinner and voted it quite smooth. But when our lively repast was over, and we faced the open again, we had a dismal foretaste of the dreary night we were condemned to pass, the seas breaking frantically over us, and the *Griffin* shivering as if she were weary of her continued battling with the storm.

For seven days and seven nights from our date

of departure from Falmouth, we had a succession of gales, and the wind was always against us. As we neared Gibraltar, we saw three great ocean steamers putting about and returning to port, unable to face the heavy sea and fierce wind. On the 29th of January we approached the rock of Gibraltar, and, according to directions, we hoisted the yellow quarantine flag and cruised about the harbour in an aimless way, no one taking any notice of us. The Commodore got tired of this, and decided to go to the new mole and anchor there. This we did, in a position not far from several other yachts, among which were Mr. Brassey's *Sunbeam* and Lord Macdonald's *Lady of the Isles*.

As none of the officials came near us, our Commodore hauled down the yellow flag and sent a boat on shore. But we were premature, for in this first-class fort they are very particular. Our boat was sent back, and Kidby, who had gone off for the letters, came back with the information that we must "wait for *praduct*," so there were no letters that evening. Next morning, January the 30th, pratique came, and soon after the captain of the port. At first he had a little of the official manner on, but that soon passed away, and he was ever afterwards most courteous and kind. The fact is we had broken through all rules; first, in having anchored without permission near the new mole, and second, in sending a boat on shore before receiving pratique.

It was Sunday morning, and the rain poured incessantly. Still we went to the cathedral, and the strange sensation never left me that the whole building was tossing on a stormy sea. This feeling was so strong that I had to hold on to the back of the bench in front of me.

On our return on board, my dear old friend and comrade, Lieutenant-Colonel H. G. Moore, V.C., Major 93rd (Sutherland) Highlanders, came to see me. It was a pleasure meeting him again, and, as I warmly shook his hand, how many scenes came back to my memory! When I got command of my old regiment, the Connaught Rangers, in 1864, I offered the adjutancy to Moore, which he accepted, and he held that post as long as I remained in the 88th Regiment. Since then his career has been along a path of glory and honour, and it was with pride and pleasure that I met him again after some years of absence.

That feeling of brotherhood which existed in old days when a regiment was a home, and the officers formed a large and happy family bound together by bonds of friendship and *esprit de corps*, must necessarily now be extinct. The lieutenant of to-day cannot look forward to serve probably a lifetime under the colours of the regiment to which he has been first appointed, and in due time to command it, as was my happy lot. The fiat has gone forth, and the old *esprit de corps* must pass away. God grant that other evils caused by short service may not be added to the total abolition of " pride in one's regiment " which was the boast of officers and men before these radical changes were introduced. The officers and men may be equally good as those of the "old army," but it is impossible that the same love for their regiments can exist in the breasts of men who one day are in one corps and the next in another. I belonged to the "old army," which was proud to be called royal, and which looked to the sovereign as the fountain of honour and reward.

Under Moore's guidance, we visited the galleries of Gibraltar, which are burrowed in the rock. As the rain poured without stopping, it was a damp expedition.

Owing to the severe weather we had experienced, the whole yacht was very damp, so the Commodore and Princess and the whole of their party took up quarters at the Royal Hotel. Time passed merrily enough in the society of old and new friends belonging to the different regiments quartered at Gibraltar.

One morning we embarked on board the steamer which plies between Gibraltar and Algesiras. The day was fine, and a fresh breeze swept away all clouds and mist. We took about an hour to reach the opposite coast, and, after landing at the pier, proceeded to the hotel, where luncheon and excellent Amontillado fortified us greatly. The Princess, attended by the Commodore, Susan, Kildonan, and Parker, mounted on donkeys, rode to some orange-groves a few miles from the town. They had several amusing adventures. One of their long-eared chargers lay down when crossing a stream, and another one fell while passing over a boggy place.

Miss Hare, my wife and I, having procured a guide, explored the town, which is a clean Spanish city. The streets are hard to walk along, but the cathedral is an interesting building in the piazza.

Having always understood that Algesiras was **a** great place for bull-fights, **we** told our guide to take us **to** the arena, which is quite new, and was now in solitude, for the games do not take place till July. A man came and conducted us all over **it,** explaining with great gusto the names and uses of the different holes and corners where the matadors escaped when the enraged bull attacked them. He became quite eloquent in his descriptions, but the impression left on **my mind** was that every advantage was given to **the** men, and that poor "Toro" was treated with the greatest cruelty, and had no chance.

We left the building, and proceeded **to** an esplanade overlooking the sea, where we remained some time, fanned by the breeze, enjoying the view of the rock in the distance, and watching the white-sailed feluccas flitting to and fro.

The Princess, having returned, collected her

followers, and we embarked in a launch sent for the Commodore by the Peninsular and Oriental Company. We steamed back to Gibraltar, where the Commodore and I were engaged to dine with the 93rd Highlanders.

The yacht having been declared ready, we re-embarked in her. Several dinner-parties were given on board, and the evening always ended with music, for there was a good piano in the *Griffin*, and the Princess had a sweet voice. Parker also sang many good songs. At a quarter to twelve on Friday night, February the 4th, after one of these pleasant parties, we said farewell to Moore. The anchor was weighed, and we started for Malaga. Kildonan had left us a day or two before on a visit to Granada and the Alhambra, and was to rejoin us at Malaga.

We had a good passage, and anchored again at half-past seven on the morning of February the 5th. After luncheon we landed and sauntered through the town. Malaga is a most thriving place. There is a look of business in the streets, which were crowded with carts and carriages. We paid a visit to a merchant in the hope of seeing the

Malaga raisins packed in boxes, but we were too late.

We went to see the fine old cathedral, and, having had chocolate at the hotel, we returned on board. The only disagreeable thing in Malaga was the dust, which flew in clouds and nearly blinded us.

Soon after our return on board, Kildonan appeared, after a most pleasant visit to the Alhambra; so that same night we put to sea again. The sea ran high, and the wind blew very fresh. We made for Oran, on the coast of Africa. On Sunday, the 6th of February, the Commodore read prayers. A fine breeze was blowing, and we coasted along the African shore. We passed Habaler Rocks, which looked like the mainland. In the evening, as the night was coming on, we made the narrow entrance to the harbour, and shortly afterwards anchored in the snug port of Oran.

After breakfast we landed at Oran, which is a busy French port. We walked up a steep ascent to the esplanade, which overlooks the harbour. There are some trees planted on it, and a great number of benches are conveniently placed for those who seek shelter and rest. A fine bandstand is also erected.

On a high hill which rises abruptly above the town is a fort, near which on a rock is a shrine to the Virgin. In it is a statue of Mary, who appears as if blessing the buildings and harbour which nestle at her feet.

We passed through dirty, smelly streets which are built on the side of a hill. Several houses were marked by a bloody hand, an emblem which, we were informed, gave warning that fever and other diseases prevailed in these dwellings. Oran is said to be a very feverish place, the people looking pallid and weak. On the top of the mountain is a fort, into which we tried to enter, but were stopped by French sentries; so we retraced our steps, and, having refreshed ourselves at a café near the landing-place, we were not sorry to return on board again. In consequence of its unhealthiness, Oran is not an inviting spot to remain at, but our visit to it was an amusing interlude in our voyage.

We steamed away at two p.m., with a strong north-west blowing and a lively sea. We danced over the waves till evening, when the sun set in gorgeous beauty. After dinner I sat on the deck and smoked a cigar. What a starlit sky and restless sea! There is an ecstatic feeling comes over me when bounding along with a fresh breeze filling the sails. But the moon sank and the wind changed, and I left the deck **not** quite satisfied with the look of the weather.

We coasted along the African shore all night. In the morning the wind was dead against us, but **wo** steamed against the current, and we had a good view of the mountains, and with a glass saw plainly the Christian's tomb, a high monumental edifice much venerated by the Arabs.

About one in the afternoon **we** entered the harbour **of** Algiers, and anchored near a Russian man-of-war, *The Duke of Edinburgh*.

The appearance of the **town is** most dazzling, for the houses are all white. **We** landed on the morning of February the 9th, and walked through the arcades, which remind one of Paris. Indeed the new part of the town is quite French. **As** we sauntered along, we were struck with the French look of everything; the names of the streets were all French.

One of our party pointed out a grand building, and informed us that it was a *fort*, for on the gate was written "Sonnez Fort"—"Ring loudly." The shouts of laughter with which this news was received must have astonished the grave-looking Arabs who were loitering near. It recalled to me a similar mistake made by a brother-officer of mine called "Joe," who, when we were quartered in Malta, informed us that the best man in the island for gloves was Gants, from Paris.

Leaving the French part of the town, we went into the Arab quarter. The climb is very steep, up a street of many steps. Everything is different here from what it is in the other part of the city. The shops are more Oriental, and the divans full of Arabs. At the summit of the hill we came to the old palace and citadel of the Dey of Algiers, now in possession of the French, and by a different road we descended to the harbour again.

In the afternoon, when it became cooler, we landed and hired one of the little open carriages of the place, drawn by a pair of clever ponies, and had a most pleasant excursion to Bou-Zaree, by Mustapha through El-Biar. It was a lovely **drive up a** steep mountain, among fields of geraniums and trees just beginning to bud in the early spring. The sun had nearly **set, and it** became cold, as we turned to go home. **The** road down the mountain zigzagged **in a** truly French manner. We trotted at a good pace along a rough road, and finally arrived safely in the Place du Gouvernement.

The Jardin d'Essai is well worth a visit. It is situated near the sea, about half an hour's drive from the town. Every species of palm-tree grows there, and, owing to the climate and the care taken by those in charge, the whole garden is **a** most interesting place, and **we** wandered with pleasure through the green alleys down to the shore of the Mediterranean, whose beach there is composed of nothing but shells.

On two different occasions I drove there. **The** first time was on a calm and beautiful afternoon; the second, a strong breeze was blowing the dust in clouds, but, on entering the gardens, all was very pleasant.

The captain of the Russian man-of-war, **who**

had called in our absence, left his card. On it was written:

"*Capitaine Paul Novissilsky,*
                Frégate 'Duc d'Edimbourg.'"

The Commodore returned his visit, and asked him to dinner. The gallant officer's English was not of the best, for when the Commodore invited him to feed on board the yacht he replied, "I have not been so well, I cannot eat, but I *can sit under the table*." He was a cheerful man, and full of talk.

Having handed the Princess to dinner on the occasion of his honouring us with his company, when we were all seated, in walked two good-looking Russian sailors, bearing a huge basket of flowers, which they presented to the Princess in the name of their captain. Next morning he sent his steam-launch, and placed it at our disposal. The young officer in charge was Prince Bores Galetzine. We embarked, and proceeded to the old harbour, landing near the dungeons where the prisoners were confined during the time of the Algerian pirates. Dark, dismal prisons, whose walls must often have re-echoed with sounds of anguish and woe. Owing to the continual improvements made in the harbour, these old temples of cruelty are vanishing away.

In the evening the Russian frigate was lit up with magnetic lights, most useful for discovering the approach of boats at night.

CHAPTER II.

PROGRESS OF OUR CRUISE

MALTA—OLD REMINISCENCES—THE NEW FLEET—STORY OF A BELL—
BORDELLA—THE GOVERNOR'S PALACE—A MORNING CALL—A PECULI
ARITY OF THE MEDITERRANEAN—SEA COOK—A FINE MORNING AT
SEA—ANCHORED OFF CYPRUS—QUAINT TRADITION—CHAPEL OF ST
LAZARUS—ANCIENT ENGLISH FONT—LANDSCENES AT SEA—H. M. S.
"FIREBRAND"—TRADITION OF OMAR—ALEXANDRETTA—A SPORTING
SAIL—A STORMY DAY

CHAPTER II.

AFTER passing a few pleasant days at Algiers, finally, on the 11th of February, at midnight, we put to sea, which, as soon as we got outside the bay, became very rough, the breeze freshening and the wind whistling through the rigging. It blew so fiercely that some of us would willingly have tried to put into Tunis, but the Commodore wisely held on, and we flew before the gale, going thirteen knots. We heard afterwards at Malta that the gunboat *Decoy* was out in this storm near Tunis, and that the captain was washed from her bridge and drowned. What is man when fighting with the elements? The good angels watched over us, and, on the afternoon of Sunday, February the 13th, we were abeam of Pantaleria. The moon shone brightly, and the big waves followed after us, the *Griffin* tearing along as if avoiding the too near approach of the breaking sea.

The morning of the 14th of February found us still going merrily before the strong breeze, but a steamer which had left Malta made bad weather of it, for the waters seemed to wash right over her. The signal-station at Gozo asked our number as we dashed past.

We coasted the island of Malta, and at one p.m. entered the harbour of Valetta. The surf was dashing high over San Elmo Point, but we went on till we arrived at Isola, where we anchored near that noble fleet of ironclads under the command of Sir Beauchamp Seymour, and close to several yachts. Malta was full of old memories to me, for I began my soldiering in foreign parts at Fort Ricasoli. The bright sky, the sunshine, the actual smell of the air, recalled old times.

We had not been long anchored before my wife's nephew, a midshipman in the flag-ship *Alexandra*, came to welcome us. We chartered a shore boat belonging to "Bubbly Joe," son of our old regimental boatman, and landed at Nix Mangiare Stairs. But everything is changed now. In former times there was **no** way of getting into Strada Reale except **by** the **very** steep stairs called Nix Mangiare. These stairs received the name after the battle of Navarino, when many beggars used to sit near there and say, "Nix mangiare since the battle of Navarin." Why they had been without food since that particular date, I never could discover. **Now a** fine road comes down **to the** landing-place, on which carriages are driven in considerable numbers.

We hired two, and drove for a long distance. A small plantation of trees has been planted near Florian, and has received the grand-sounding name of the New Forest. When the proposal was first made to have these trees, a deputation of Maltese waited on the Governor, and prayed of him not to sanction the planting of **the** forest, as it would be a harbour for brigands.

The cold was very great during the whole **of** our stay in the island. Once we went on board the *Alexandra*, and were courteously received **by** the admiral, who had a bear on board, a great pet, but no respecter of persons, for it gambolled playfully up to its master and seized him by the leg. **It** is difficult to be dignified under such circumstances, but the gallant officer was equal to the occasion, and turned to a small midshipman and coolly said, "Tell some one to take away this bear." Easier said than done. The poor boy mumbled, in a great fright, "Pooa fello, come! pooa fello, come!" But the bear refused to release the captured leg.

At length a flight of lieutenants, midshipmen, sailors, and marines extricated the admiral from his unpleasant position, while the bear rolled away apparently delighted, and laid hold of one of the ladies of our party in the same affectionate manner. Another flight of lieutenants, midshipmen, sailors, and marines, headed by the admiral, got her free, and we all, without losing any time, went up on the poop, where we were safe.

We visited all the decks of this wonderful ship. The powerful ordnance, the enormous engines, give one a feeling of surprise and awe difficult to describe. Memory recalls the war-vessels of bygone days. How beautiful they were, sailing with a grace these ponderous demons of war never can attain!

On our return on deck, we found that the bear had jumped overboard and pursued some of the

Maltese boats which hover round a man-of-war. Bruin went too far, however, for he exposed himself to considerable risk, and he endeavoured to climb up on a buoy; but his weight was too great, and he fell back into the water. He was evidently growing weaker, and everyone on board was becoming anxious on account of him. Two men went off in a small boat to save the poor animal clinging with desperation **to** the buoy. The boat approached. It was so small that, **if** the sailors were not very careful, there was danger that the **frail** craft would **be** upset. But the bear was not quite so lively as he had been a short time before, and they got him into the dingey without much difficulty. He at once proceeded to shake himself vigorously, a process which wet his deliverers to the skin. **On** arriving on board the *Alexandra*, he raced furiously all over the ship, and on his way embraced a Maltese washerwoman, who fainted on the spot. He tore into shreds the trousers of a marine who went to the help of the woman, and when we left the vessel he was flying everywhere, pursued by sailors and marines, now really anxious to catch him and chain him up.

The Princess went often to the opera, attended by some of us. The musical attraction was not great, for the singing was wretched, but the boxes and stalls were generally well filled by the *élite* and fashion of the island. The Princess and her party were entertained at luncheon by Sir Beauchamp Seymour, after which we all went to the racecourse to see a match at polo. We visited all the sights in Malta; but these are so well known that it is needless to describe them.

Once Susan, Kildonan, my wife and I landed on the Burmola side of the harbour. Burmola was the original city before Valetta was built, and is much more picturesque. We passed old-fashioned houses, and crossed in a boat to the dockyard side. We pulled close to the *Decoy*, whose captain was lost in that gale off Tunis. On reaching the opposite landing-place, we went through many ancient gates to the Inquisitors' Palace, an old place in which I had occupied quarters for many months in former years.

The Inquisitors' Palace has been used for a long time as officers' quarters, but was now empty, owing to a change in the strength of the garrison. We knocked at the big gate, which was opened by an intelligent private of the 26th Cameronians, who ushered us in, and I took my wife straight to my old quarters, which were little altered since I occupied them many years ago. Most of **my** old comrades who were quartered **with** me in these barracks have, alas! passed **away.** Some rest in the West Indies, while others sleep in their honoured graves on **the** heights of Sebastopol and the plains **of** India. But, leaving old memories behind us, **we proceeded** on our walk to Fort San Angelo.

We remained at Malta till Sunday, February the 20th, when we steamed away against a heavy sea. We were sorry to part with our midshipman, who came with us till we left the harbour and had passed Ricasoli, and then dropped into "**Bubbly Joe's**" boat, which was hove alongside.

The wind was in the east, and dead against us. During the night the sea was very rough. Monday the 21st broke fine, **but** the wind increased to a gale, which lasted all night. Tuesday the 22nd it moderated a little, but during the day it came on to blow harder than ever, and dead against us. On Wednesday the 23rd we sighted **land,** which proved to be the coast of Greece, near

Capo Matapan. For a short time we were under the lee of Cerigo, but it blew heavier than ever, and we ran down the western coast of Candia in as strong a gale and as big a sea as we had encountered in any of our former experiences.

We changed our course, and got under the shelter of Candia. What a marvellous alteration! The wind howled and shrieked, but the high land of Crete protected us, and we were in smooth water. We ran along the southern coast till we reached Makri-Zalo Bay, where we anchored for the night, peacefully and quietly, although the storm-fiend roared above us. How pleasant that evening was! The natives lit fires on the shore, apparently to attract our attention; but we heeded them not, although they shouted at us, whether in welcome or defiance, we knew not and cared not. The sailors had a good night's rest, and I can answer for myself I slept like a top.

In the morning we started again. Mount Ida showed a snowy crest crowned with dark clouds; but the gale had moderated, and the sea was going down in that wonderful manner peculiar to the Mediterranean, which rises one moment in fury and in a short time becomes smoother and smoother.

Our cook was a facetious character, besides being a first-rate artist. During the gale off Candia, my wife addressed some kindly words to him as he passed her on the deck. To her question if he had ever seen worse weather he replied, "Oh, this is nothink, ma'am, *this is nuss*," and, on her asking him if he was not often wet in the galley, he answered, "Yes, ma'am; if not soused with cold water I ham with 'ot!" A pleasant time he must have there.

It was seven in the morning when we bid adieu to Candia, a strong wind blowing; we were going eleven knots. We sailed most pleasantly over a dark blue sea, and could see the island of Rhodes in the far distance. The cook informed the Princess he had been in a cyclone on his way to India, and had escaped. "So, ma'am," added he, "'nil desperandum!'"

The day passed in reading, writing, and walking on the dry deck, in the warmth of the sun, which when it set sank in unclouded glory. The night was beautiful and calm, and our hearts were filled with joy and gratitude. Next morning was one of those which come back to one's memory even after years are passed. It was, in fact, the hour I like the best, the sun shining brightly on the blue sea, just rippled by a favouring breeze. There was a buoyancy in the air, for the day was young, and the weather had not become coarse and wild. The canaries were full of song, and even Wallace the dog appeared less bored and more content than usual. The ladies came out on deck looking fresh and well. The Commodore was tracing our course on his chart, and the captain was full of glee, for he had suffered severely from toothache, and my wife had given him a cure for it.

There is something heavenly in a fine morning at sea. The breakfast-bell sounded, and we met in radiant good-humour. At twelve, noon, we were fifty-two miles from the nearest point of Cyprus, so the day slipped away into evening, and, when night came on, the brightest stars hung out like lamps in the heavens, and the *Griffin* gently pushed her way through a sea of glistening phosphorescent light.

On Sunday, February the 27th, we anchored off

Larnaca, in the island of Cyprus, a very **insecure** anchorage. The appearance of the town is **not** imposing from the sea, and the whole place has a ruinous aspect. After luncheon we got pratique and landed. The assistant commissioner, **Mr.** Cobham, received us most courteously at the consular house near the landing-place. **He** kindly accompanied us in our walk, and showed us the various sights of the place.

Passing through the bazaar, we came to the Greek Church **of** St. Lazarus, where tradition says Lazarus is buried. We were quaintly informed "that, after Lazarus was raised from the dead, he did **not** *get on with his friends*, so they sent him to Cyprus, where he died." There are some interesting tombs, in good preservation, of members of old English families, Palmer and Barton. The date is A.D. 15—, and the arms of both these families are very well cut on the marble tombs.

The Princess made many purchases of old curiosities which had been dug up in various parts of the island. One beautiful glass tear-bottle, the date of which was at least 200 B.C., shortly after it was brought on board was knocked over and broken, and, before I could rescue the pieces, they were thrown into the sea.

We left Cyprus at half-past three, when it began to rain, which deprived us of the view of Famagosta promised to us after passing the point beyond Larnaca. The sea was calm, and there was no gale. The Commodore read prayers in the saloon, and all attended whose duties did not prevent them.

Before we arrived at Cyprus, we were all on deck, when Susan exclaimed, "There is a snipe!" We were far from land, and the poor wanderer must have been borne away on an easterly gale. It fluttered round our ship, and at length came on board and was caught. Susan was most tenderly careful of it, and the Scotch gamekeeper promised to look after it; but the poor bird was too weak, and died. It is wonderful how far land-birds will fly over the sea.

Once I was in command of a wing of the Connaught Rangers proceeding to India round the Cape. We were going merrily before a breeze, some five hundred miles from any land. I was seated on the deck of the good ship *Ulysses*, read-

ing, when suddenly a little land-bird flew into my
bosom and nestled itself in the folds of my waistcoat. Everyone on board did all they could to
save the life of the poor little wanderer. The
soldiers brought a huge hen-coop, in which they
made a nest for it. It was **of no** avail, the worn-
out little traveller died.

On the 28th of February, at eight in the morning, we were passing Cape Hazal Khanzar, near
the entrance **to the Bay of** Scandaroon. The
wall of mountains was covered with snow, and
the sharp air breathed **of** frost. **As we** approached Alexandretta, the miserable town near
a swamp became plainer to view. A man-of-war
which was lying at anchor proved **to** be H.M.S.
Coquette, Commander Burr, and **a** merchant
steamer was preparing **for** sea. The **snow-**
covered mountains towered over the mean-looking
village, and overhead was the blue sky, and
beneath the deceitful Mediterranean Sea.

In process of time, I landed with the Commodore, and proceeded to call on the English Consul,
Signor Cottoni; but he was in bed, so we went to
the Italian Consul's house, but he also was *au lit*.
What could it mean? were they all ill? At length

the British Consul appeared, and, with many apologies, explained that a marriage had taken place in his family the day before, and that the ball to celebrate the nuptials had kept him up till seven in the morning. Nothing could exceed the civility, courtesy, and hospitality of these consuls.

We made the acquaintance of the officers of the *Coquette*, and a real friendship sprang up between the two ships, not only among ourselves, but also between the two crews. The officers of the *Coquette* had made a lawn-tennis ground on the sandy plain above the beach, and often afterwards, when the shades of evening were closing round us while a hardly-contested game was being played, the on-lookers were drinking tea and eating cakes provided by the hospitable *Coquettes*. Sometimes the kettle was upset and the tea somewhat strong, but the fun was greater owing to these mishaps.

Not very far from this impromptu tennis-ground are two pillars at the extreme end of a cape, the dark shade of whose wooded banks are clearly seen in the rays of light cast by the fast setting sun. These pillars mark where Jonah was thrown on shore by the whale. There is

more apparent truth in this tradition than in most
stories of the kind, for Jonah was going from
Joppa to Tarsus, and this would naturally be his
route, for Tarsus is at the end of the bay.

The sunsets were most magnificent. In the
glowing light we could see the field of Issus,
where Alexander fought Darius. When the sun
was disappearing in grandeur unspeakable, the
whole air was filled **by** the noise of millions of
frogs, whose loud music proclaimed the proximity
of fever-laden marshes. The society of Alexandretta, the seaport of Scandaroon, is composed
entirely of consuls and their families, most truly
hospitable people, who did all they could to be
courteous and attentive. Several dances were
given by them, **to** which the *Coquettes* and *Griffins*
were always invited.

Our Commodore, being very anxious to show
some sport to Kildonan and Parker, had made
inquiries, but had received a not very satisfactory account. The best ground was near Ayas
Bay; so on the 2nd of March, at four in the
morning, we left Scandaroon, and made Ayas
Bay at half-past six.

The bay is enclosed by a low-lying country.

To the westward of where we were anchored is a high hill, on the other side of which Tarsus is situated. An ancient castle in ruins stands near the entrance of the bay, noble and dignified in appearance, but weak and useless from old age. Many flocks of sheep and droves of cattle were feeding near the shore. We landed on this Asia Minor coast at a stair cut in the soft rock by the men of H.M.S. *Monarch*, who had passed many weeks in this bay. The banks above were thickly covered by prickly bushes, but at their base grew flowers in great profusion, anemones and cyclamen. The balmy, fresh air was most enjoyable, and the sunset was wonderful in its beauty.

For several days preparations had been going on for a shooting excursion into the country. Everything being ready on the 3rd of March, the three sportsmen, the Commodore, Kildonan, and Parker, together with M'Gregor, paraded in the early morning on the deck of the *Griffin*. They were to be accompanied by two native shikarrees, one of whom was described as a good man, but the other as a sneak. It had come on to blow hard, and, as the sea was getting up, our sportsmen had rather a difficulty in getting into the cutter. Apparently they did not mind, or could not help, what part of their person arrived first in the boat. Their rifles, guns, and baggage had been sent on shore to go round by land, on horses and camels, to meet the party at the end of a twenty miles' sail. Five sailors went with the cutter, which reduced the number of our crew very much.

We saw them start on their stormy voyage, and heard no more of them till next day. In the meantime, one of those sudden squalls from the mountains came down upon us; the attention of everyone was occupied hauling down the awning, and we were five men short. The lifeboat had been lowered that morning to take the baggage on shore, and was still in the water. A terrible scene of confusion ensued; everyone hauling and pulling, but without being able to do much. The lifeboat was stove in, and, when at length she was raised on deck, she was sorely crippled. The captain gave orders to let go another anchor, and all day a series of squalls more or less heavy continued. At sunset it blew a strong gale from S.S.E., which moderated at midnight, and at sunrise the sea was calm, as the wind had veered round to the north, and in the bay, where we anchored, we were sheltered, but our anxiety about the cutter was great.

Kidby went on shore in the dingy, in hopes of getting some news, and returned with a native, who brought a note to the Princess from the Commodore, informing her that they were safe, but, owing to the difficulties they encountered, the men and the cutter would not return for three days, and demanding provisions and clothes to be sent for them. All this was done, and the supplies were dispatched under the charge of the native who had brought the note.

So we were left to occupy our time as well as we could. That day passed, as days will pass, whether in solitude and grief or in happiness and joy. We could not land, as not only was the cutter away and the lifeboat a wreck, but our hands were short. When night came the stars shone bright and beautiful, and the young moon lit up the calm and treacherous sea.

The morning of Saturday was full of sunshine, but cold. The rain poured and the thunder rolled in the hills, but the bay was quiet and smooth. Sunday, March the 6th, in the absence of the Commodore, I read prayers, and the day passed peacefully, although we were exposed to thunderstorms and squalls which kept up in the mountains, and all this time we could not land.

The next day the cutter returned with the five men, who looked as if they had undergone some rough work. The morning they left the yacht it blew a strong gale, and they had to leave the **bay** and go out into the open before they could enter the river Pyramus, up which they were to sail for twenty miles. The river is broad and deep, except at the entrance, which is very shallow. They were obliged to **take** out everything from the boat to lighten it, and, when they got over the bar, they reloaded again. The strong gale favoured them once they were into the deep river, enabling the cutter to face the current, which was very strong against them. The Commodore and his party had seen many wild boars, and had killed several. Two fine ones were brought back by the sailors; besides which they had captured numerous tortoises of all sizes, from the dimensions of a large plate to that of a small saucer.

As every sailor on board possessed a tortoise,

each man, in order to distinguish his property, a few days afterwards painted the backs of these very stupid pets; one appearing with a red, blue, and white back, while the shell of another was painted black and white, according to the taste of the owner.

As soon as the returning boat was seen approaching, the captain ordered steam to be got up, and shortly afterwards we started for Scandaroon, and in three hours anchored near the *Coquette*, a bright moon lighting up the snow-covered hills.

Captain Burr came on board to welcome us. During our absence at Ayas Bay, he had made an official visit to Larnaca, where, while we were lying snug in Ayas Bay, they encountered a perfect storm. The green seas washed over them when at anchor, and their best boat was smashed to pieces. Verily the Mediterranean is not the calm lake some people fondly suppose it to be.

CHAPTER III.

IN EASTERN CLIMES.

WALK TO LA FONTAINE—ALEXANDRETTA—THE SHIP OF THE DESERT—MADAME GUYOUN'S MOTHER DANSANTE—GUN PRACTICE IN PAYAS BAY—A PILGRIMAGE TO ANTIOCH—THE BEILAN PASS—CURRENTLY FREQUENTED BY BRIGANDS—THE SYRIAN GATES—HOSPITABLY ENTERTAINED BY A JEW—ANTIOCH—THE CHURCH OF ST. JOHN—PUBLIC BATHS—PALACE BUILT BY ANTIOCHUS—GRATEFUL OLD LADY.

CHAPTER III

HAVING returned to Alexandretta on the night of Monday, March the 7th, we landed next day. My wife and I walked to La Fontaine, to reach which we had to pass through the town by the narrow, ill-paved streets, and then to cross the swamp.

La Fontaine is a fine spring of the purest water. It flows into a tank, which is surrounded by a wall, but when it leaves this confined space it spreads itself over the low ground between it and Alexandretta, and forms a marsh where frogs are continually croaking, and which is the cause of deadly fever. By the expenditure of a few thousand pounds this swamp might be drained, and the value of the land would repay the outlay. But decay and ruin seem everywhere to be the effect of Turkish misrule.

Alexandretta might be made a first-rate harbour by building a mole as a protection against the only wind which is severely felt. Except Haifa, there is no other good place of anchorage on the Syrian coast.

Just outside the town, near the *Coquette's* lawn-tennis ground, there is a camp where the camels arriving from Aleppo laden with goods generally halt. It was a curious sight, watching the "ships of the desert" returning to their station in the evening. During the day they go out to feed on green leaves, and, when sunset approaches, long strings of them are seen coming home. Some of them look quite cheerful, and canter along in a most ungainly manner; while others walk calmly and deliberately, reminding one of a fine lady sailing across a room. When a railway is made to Aleppo, the complaining camel's "occupation's gone." Till that event takes place, however, the moaning, grumbling animal must still be employed.

The Princess entertained the officers of the *Coquette* at dinner, after which the piano was brought up from the saloon, and we had dancing on deck. I had retired into the deck cabin with a prize, the latest newspaper. Once I tried to get out, but found the passage blocked by the piano, so I resumed the study of my paper. But I had visitors. The active young officers of the *Cayuette* came in at the window, and after a little disappeared by the same way. I was quite flattered at their kindness in coming to see me during my imprisonment, till I discovered that their visit was not altogether to me, but partially to the refreshments, which had got confined with me in the deck saloon.

Madame Cottoni also gave a *soirée dansante*, which was a great success, and everyone seemed pleased; but dancing a quadrille at Alexandretta is really hard work. The Greek Consul, a fine, soldier-like man, generally took command; he shouted out the different figures to be danced, and it was interesting to observe how cleverly his orders were obeyed. But the last figure was a puzzler, and to a looker-on it seemed rather a romp. All kinds of different manœuvres were executed in obedience to the word of command, and the quadrille lasted for at least half an hour.

On the 10th of March we started for Ayas Bay to meet the sportsmen. We anchored at nine in the morning, and the shooting-party returned during the day. Though sunburnt and unshaved, they all looked well, but evidently had been hard worked. The sport had been very good so far as pigs went. They brought the carcases of two boars, besides several other victims of their skill as shots. Poor Wallace the dog had been accidentally shot. While running mute after a boar which got up in the jungle, a bullet aimed at the object of his pursuit unfortunately hit him, and he fell dead.

That same evening we returned to Scandaroon, and a most unpleasant voyage we had. The wind and sea got up, and the *Griffin* showed her tendency to roll in the most aggravating way.

From this date, the 11th of March, time fled fast at Alexandretta. What with walks, lawn-tennis, and dinner-parties, it was difficult to believe that we were anchored off the "most unwholesome part on the Syrian coast." The weather, too, was variable, fine weather alternating with storms and gales, smooth seas with rough and boisterous tempests.

On Monday, March the 14th, we were all invited on board the *Coquette*, where a large party of the consuls, their wives, sisters, and children, were assembled. Captain Burr had particularly requested that the children should *not* be brought, but I suppose the *not* had escaped the notice of the fond mothers, for they all were there.

The most remarkable peculiarity of these foreign ladies was that they became sea-sick the moment they came on board, and in no way concealed their symptoms, but were very open in the expression of them. The men shouted, sang, and smoked cigarettes, and seemed to enjoy themselves very much.

"Come to my cabin, we shall have a quiet talk," said Captain Burr to me; but, on his opening the door, there was a stout lady extended on his sofa, with a large bucket near her!

When we approached Beyas Bay, gun-practice began, and the foreign ladies screamed and were sick alternately. We landed near an old castle which had been built by the Crusaders, and, climbing a steep bank, we walked about half a mile to the village of Beyas, where the Kaimakan had placed his house at our disposal. Four of us sauntered away to the old castle, now used as a prison, and were shown up to the top of a

E 2

tower, from which we saw, assembled in a court below, about sixty prisoners, who shouted and yelled as they gazed up at us, begging for "backsheesh." We threw some small silver change among them, and the struggle that ensued was like that of wild beasts.

After wandering through the bazaar and inspecting the remains of the old Roman road, we returned on board. Once more the foreign ladies resumed their morning occupation, whilst the others danced on the deck to the music so sweetly given by "the doctor" on the piano, lent for the occasion by the Princess.

The sun had set and the frogs were chanting their evening song when we got back to Scandaroon, and the *Coquette* anchored in her old position.

On the morning of the 15th of March, we had no sooner left our berths than we began to rush up and down the companion-ladder in the energetic manner so emblematical of a proposed trip. There were, in fact, two different parties, the one consisting of Susan, Kildonan, my wife, and myself, bound for Antioch; while the other, which included the Commodore and Parker, was proceeding on an expedition against bears among the mountains. Landed at the wooden pier, we were soon assembled at the English Consul's house, where a string of miserable-looking ponies were seen in every kind of pensive attitude. These poor beasts, however, proved themselves, when warmed to their work, to be the most sure-footed animals in creation, and carried us over rocky paths and muddy plains without the slightest accident.

Monsieur Cottoni, with his usual courteous kindness, had made every arrangement for our comfort, providing the two ladies with side-saddles and sending two of his own men with us. Constantin, who spoke French, acted as our dragoman and interpreter, while the other man, the gaily-caparisoned "cavass," armed to the teeth and mounted on a free-going Arab, curvetted in front of the line. The four travellers followed in single file, the rear being brought up by Constantin, mounted on a baggager, and followed by another pony for the baggage, and a donkey, whose wonderful feats of agility were the surprise of us, the pilgrims to Antioch.

We scrambled and slipped over the roughly-paved streets of Alexandretta, and, having left the town and crossed the swamp, whose million frogs were silent in this morning hour, we passed La Fontaine and turned to the left, leaving the broad, uneven road for a bridle-path, and soon commenced the ascent of the Beilân Pass.* The track was one mass of rocks, with occasional bits of the old Roman road, and here and there a piece of the thickest mud; but our ponies struggled on, and for three hours we were still ascending, and at length arrived at the village of Beilân, which is situated in a gorge. We descended a very steep incline before we entered the village. Its narrow streets are badly paved, but it is a picturesque spot, and the Italian Consul has a house here, where he passes the unhealthy months.

There are bits of an aqueduct to be seen here, and the traces of an old Roman road. This place

* "It was by this pass that Alexander the Great entered Syria after defeating Darius on the plains of Issus below. It was along this road Barnabas went from Antioch to Tarsus to seek Saul (Acts xi, 25). It was along it the Crusaders defiled after their weary march through Asia Minor, and along it caravans pass and re-pass between Aleppo and Scandaroon."—Murray's "Syria."

has been identified as the "Syrian Gates." The road ascends for about a mile, and to our surprise we came on a most excellent highway; but this did not last long. A considerable sum had been collected **to** make a good road, but, as usual, the most part of the money got into the Turkish officials' pockets, and so no progress was made. At the top of the pass the way divides, one branch going to Aleppo, the other descending through the "Defiles of Amanus" to Antioch; the latter the one by which we went. We had two muleteers, who were armed with pistols and swords.

The country through which we were now passing has been for centuries noted as the abode of brigands, and the shepherds of Amanus have been always notorious. When we arrived at a certain point, the muleteers fired off their pistols twice—I daresay, as a signal that **we had** paid blackmail by hiring them.

The scenery was wild in the extreme, and the path looked like the bed of a torrent. When we arrived at the foot of one mountain, we generally had to cross a deep stream, and then toil up another hill. Some very stiff bits of mountain-climbing we and our ponies had to get over before we came in view of the lake, with its marshy border, called "Bahr-el-Abyed," "The White Lake," and also "The Lake of Antioch." After sighting it from the heights, we descended to a stream, leaving the ruins of a large fortress on our right, and were glad to halt at the khan on the other side. No doubt our ponies were as glad of the rest as we were, after five hours' continual march.

Kildonan exerted himself to get luncheon out of the basket, for we only allowed ourselves half an hour's halt, and then we were in our saddles and off again.

For some miles after leaving the khan we rode over level, grassy ground, then we came again on the old Roman road, which was difficult for the ponies to keep their feet on. It is about four feet wide, and is composed of smooth, round stones. We always rode beside it when we could; but the peculiarity of the ground for miles, on the journey to Antioch, was the sticky mud of which it was composed. The ponies sank in it in many places when they diverged from the slippery, painful stones. The sun set while we had still many weary miles of this muddy road between us and Antioch. In the growing darkness we lost our way, but the gallant ponies floundered in the marsh, and scrambled up banks and over ditches. At length the bridge over the Orontes was seen in the increasing gloom, and, once across it, we were in Antioch. We turned to the right, and at half-past eight in the evening we dismounted at the hospitable Jew's house, where we were expected.

The venerable old man was dressed in a long, sky-blue sort of dressing-gown lined with white fur. His grey hair appeared under a curious-shaped cap, and his handsome face and graceful manners were very prepossessing. He ushered us into his reception-room at the end of a long corridor—a splendid, long room lined with divans, and, at the extreme end, a balcony hanging over the rushing waters of the Orontes. We were introduced to his wife and three sons and their wives, also to a son-in-law. We could not have much conversation with him, as Italian was the only European language he spoke, and, from long disuse, my Italian had become rusty, and none of the others spoke it at all; but, by dint of signs and a few words, we got on very well. Although wearied with our long thirty-three miles' ride, we men had to smoke a cigarette and drink the inevitable cup of coffee, while my wife and Susan underwent a catechetical examination from the Arabic ladies as to their families, the conversation being carried on in French. If we had then left the house, the remembrance of that benign old man would have remained as a pleasing memory; but this could not be, we had to remain all night.

Kildonan and I were shown into a bed-room in which were a bed and a cot. To reach this apartment we had to pass through an ante-room, in which the cavass and Constantin smoked and slept.

The process of dressing and washing was enlivened by the company of one or two sons of the house, who, with cigarettes in their lips, sauntered in at unexpected moments. My wife and Susan shared another room, the privacy of which was not very great, for Susan was busy buttoning her boots, when Constantin walked in and sat down. After contemplating her occupation for some time, he at length observed, between a puff of his cigarette, "Mademoiselle, you have too many buttons to your boots." The hospitality shown by all was very great, **but I** must write the truth. No words can express the dirt and filth of these rooms.

Wearied and longing for sleep, we retired to our beds. At first tired nature **sank to** rest, but, oh! the awakening! Myriads of **fleas** hopped and crawled about and pricked; but here I pause, and only add, if any soldier of the old Crimean campaign recalls to mind the inmates he met in **his** quarters there, he will understand and enter **into** the feelings of the pilgrims to Antioch.

Old Antioch **is no** more. Sieges and earthquakes wrecked the ancient city, and the new town **is** outside **the** former site. Beyond the present boundary, on the way to "Paul's Gate," " Bab Bulus," where **the** Church **of** St. John is found in a rock, ruined walls everywhere and broken pillars testify that, where now are gardens, once stood the great city of Antioch, where the followers of Christ were first named Christians, and where Paul and Barnabas dwelt so long.

The church is on the hill-side in a grotto. **We** procured the key from the Greek Papa, **and,** having been told there was no distance to walk, we started on foot, piloted by the son-in-law of our host, who spoke French fluently. He looked quite a boy, but he had risen in importance in the last two days, his wife having given birth to a son, the first grandson who had yet gladdened the eyes of our patriarchal host, though we saw any number of granddaughters.

The afternoon was very hot, and the pavement of Antioch was excessively painful to walk on. We passed through the narrow, crowded streets, objects of interest to all who gazed. Our importance was undoubted, for not only had we our own magnificently-attired cavass and dragoman, but also the cavass and janissary of our consul at Antioch. The two unveiled ladies of our party, too, were an unusual sight in far-away Syria.

We were called on to halt at the baths, and my wife and Susan were invited to enter the building to see them. We men were not permitted to accompany the ladies, as the women have exclusive possession of the baths in the afternoon, while the men occupy them before midday. We waited in the shade, and in a short time our ladies reappeared, escorted by a number of perfectly nude figures, who vanished with much affected confusion when they saw us. My wife said she thought most of the ladies of Antioch must have been in the baths, where they apparently spend their afternoons. Delighted to welcome Susan and her, they were quite disappointed because they would not remain with them for the rest of the day.

From the baths we went on, passing out of the **town** into the highway to Aleppo. Orchards lined the road, but the trees cast no shade on the glaring, uneven track. Continual strings of camels and laden ponies passed us, the men **in** charge all armed.

The Church of St. John was always "encore cinq minutes" **away.** Much we regretted not having ridden. **At last** the wall **was** reached that we had **to climb, and** our walk continued over a hard, ploughed field till we arrived at another steep ascent, **on** the top of which is **a** high wall. **Our** active guide mounted this wall, and, managing to unlock a door half-way up, he drew forth a wooden ladder, the only way of ascending to the church, which stands back in **a** grotto in the mountain side. **We** found a green enclosure, in which are several tombs, but none of any antiquity. The dome and part of the supporting pillars are very ancient; but the altar was erected by Pio Nono. A marble slab with an inscription states "that Pio Nono, &c., erected this altar in memory of St. Peter, Bishop of Antioch." To the left of the altar is a deep cavern, and our guide informed us that there is a covered way communicating with the ruins of the palace, built by Antiochus on the hill above.

How often Paul and Barnabas must have gazed on these hills from the grotto's mouth! This church on the rock is the only speaking remembrance of these old times. Remains of the walls of Antioch stretch all the way up the mountain side.

Kildonan and Susan bravely climbed to the palace, and were rewarded by the extensive view which they had from it, and the loud applause of all the people, who were much surprised at Susan's activity. I did not care for attempting such a daring feat, so my wife remained with me, and we rested for some time in a grotto near a stream enjoying the shade, and our minds occupied by the thoughts which such an interesting spot must suggest.

But the afternoon was passing, and it was time to retrace our steps. Our pleasant guide was still with us, and led us along terraces made for cultivation on the hill-side. I was rejoiced when we came on a road from which there was a fine view of Antioch.

As we descended the hill, an old woman passed carrying an earthen jar of water. We asked her for a drink, which she gladly gave, a courtesy for which my wife rewarded her with some small change. The poor old lady was most grateful, and our guide said she was much surprised, as it is not the custom in Antioch to pay for any civility.

CHAPTER IV.

EASTERN EXPERIENCES.

VISIT OF MR. MARTIN, THE MISSIONARY—THE BAZAAR AT ANTIOCH—JOURNEY TO THE GROTTO OF DAPHNE—A GROTTO AND CASCADE—THE ORONTES—MR. EDDY, THE MISSIONARY—HIS LOVELY WIFE AND HIS FAMILY—LEGEND OF THE LAKE—ASCENT OF THE RIVER OF AMANUS—THE SYRIAN GATES—THE BEILAN PASS—A SHOOTING PARTY—A VISIT TO BEILAN—A VISIT TO PARKER—QUARANTINE AT ALEXANDRIA—PROCESS OF FUMIGATION.

CHAPTER IV.

ON arriving **at** our old Jew's house, **we found** a large party assembled to congratulate our guide on the birth of a son.

In the evening Mr. Martin, a missionary, came **to** call upon us, and furnished us with much information. There are very few Christians now at Antioch, once the largest of the Seven Churches. Mr. Martin had been preaching that day in the street. His hearers were respectful and quiet, and, as he moved away, two men followed him and said, " Sir, we believe that Jesus Christ was the Son of God." With the Mahomedans he has little success. The Greek Church oppose him in every way. Those who listen to him are idolaters, who worship the sun and moon, and whose rites are secret. Mr. Martin is a bold little man, a

Scotchman by birth, and his wife is an American, and a worthy help-meet.

It is sad to hear of the misgovernment of this fine country, of which bribery is the ruling power. Justice is awarded to the highest bidder. An honest man in office cannot remain in it. The very fact of being truthful is enough to prevent him remaining in authority. He is removed, and the subservient man takes his place. This is a fact, not a surmise. The lower orders are a fine-looking, and powerful, industrious race, who, if properly governed, would cultivate the land, which is fertile even without any care.

The bazaar at Antioch reminded me of Pompeii, for up the centre of the street is that deep kind of way through which the laden animals proceed, while on each side is the paved way for foot-passengers. Crowds of armed men in picturesque costumes were lounging about the shop doors, but they did not stare rudely at our party, as would have been the case at home. They may have thought a good deal, but they did not express their sentiments; these, however, were strangers to the town who had come in from the country. The usual dwellers in the bazaar followed us in numbers, and sometimes it was difficult to get on after stopping for a moment to examine anything on the shop counters.

Kildonan made many purchases, and the interest the crowd took in his bargains was most amusing.

On the 17th of March, at eight in the morning, we assembled in front of the Jew's house, and, having been joined by Mr. Martin, we proceeded on our way to the groves of Daphne. For some miles the roads were bad, a combination of the old Roman road **and** holes of thick and sticky mud; but, as we approached Daphne, imagination recalled lanes at home. The young spring leaves were peeping forth. **In** another ten days these banks would be covered with flowers.

There are no remains of the temples erected in honour of Daphne. Even the woods and groves have all been swept away by the destroying Turk but the cascade which comes out of the rock in the grotto flows clear and pure as it did in the days of Julian the Apostate, and rushes down to the valley beneath, undefiled **by** idolatrous rites.

We scrambled up to the grotto, and there had

our luncheon. Susan and Kildonan, accompanied by Mr. Martin, departed on an exploring expedition; but my wife and I remained by the foaming torrent, and were almost sent to sleep by the sound of the rushing waters. The worst part of these expeditions is that one cannot loiter on the way, for in seemingly a very short space of time the dragoman becomes fussy, and anxious to get on. So we two toiled up a very steep path by which we had descended, as the site of the groves of Daphne is in a valley, and there waited for the explorers, who had not seen much more than we had.

Having mounted our horses, we bid adieu to Mr. Martin, who then returned to Antioch, while we continued our journey to Suweidiyeh. It was a lovely country we rode over; the paths were steep and precipitous; but our confidence in our ponies' sure-footedness was unbounded, for they never made a false step.

We crossed the Orontes, a couple of miles below Daphne, in a ferry-boat; the river here, a swiftly-flowing, deep, brown-coloured stream, is much more narrow than at Antioch. And now we passed through a valley and forded another river, rushing **to** join the Orontes. So our path continued up hill and down hill, till we reached the orchards and gardens of Suweidiyeh.

Mr. Barker, a former English Consul, built a house here, and made many gardens. He is now dead, and his dwelling is **in** ruins; **but** the orchards remain.

We were received **at a** nice-looking cottage, once the property of a well-to-do man who was in the Consular Agency; but he died, and now his widow reigns in his stead. Alas! the Turkish authorities have somehow got hold of her money, and, with tears in her eyes, she explained through Constantin that her house and property were for sale.

She most hospitably entertained us with all she had, and refused any remuneration. We had begun the dinner which Constantin and the widow's united efforts had provided; he having cooked and dressed the tough fowl, while she had concocted the various sour salads, **a** *menu* to which was added a tin of potted beef we carried with us. A table had been drawn up in front of the divan, with which the sides of the room was lined, and we sat in a row to eat, when visitors were announced, and in walked Mr. Essom, a missionary, with his two assistants. The news of our arrival had reached him, and, glad no doubt at the prospect of meeting some European strangers, he had come to welcome us to Suweidiyeh.

Mr. Essom is an American, and served during the war in the Northern Army, but now devotes his life to missionary work. His two companions were natives of the country, who, having become Christians, help him now in his labours. They remained some time with us, and, before leaving, Mr. Essom pressed us to take breakfast with him next morning, when he would make us acquainted with his wife, and show us the school under his charge. So early next morning we walked to his pretty house, situated on the brow of a hill within view of the sea.

Mrs. Essom, also an American, is a most charming woman, who for several years has turned her attention to missionary work. She was delighted to meet English ladies again, and was most kind and friendly to Susan and my wife. She told us that she never sees an American or English stranger's face, except when they take their yearly summer holidays to those places where many of the missionaries of Northern Syria have built houses, and it is the great point in their year's work meeting together and **com-paring progress.**

It was extremely interesting seeing the school and hearing the scholars read. The oldest class read English with the greatest fluency, and all of them seemed to a certain extent familiar with the language. Children of all creeds were there, almost all of whom were boarders, and many of them, Mrs. Essom told us, orphans. One nice little girl we saw, whose father and mother had died, and, she being left utterly destitute, Mrs. Essom adopted her. **We** might have spent another hour among the children, **but** time had to be thought of, so we went **to** breakfast, which was excellent. The gentle American and her fine, stalwart husband regaled us grandly. The remembrance **of** the "sally luns" will long last in our memory.

The day looked very dark and stormy, and the rain swept up from the sea. We had proposed going on to Seleucia, where Paul and Barnabas embarked; but we gave it up. So, saying farewell to our graceful hostess, we began our return march to Antioch. We diverged from our former route, and crossed over a steep ascent by a rocky road. Mr. Essom, who accompanied us for some distance, was mounted on a wild little Arab, whose great dread of a camel made him go off in a scare when we met a string of these animals on the road, laden with goods for Antioch.

Soon after Mr. Essom had taken leave of us, we came to the banks of the same river we had crossed going to Suweidiyeh, where we halted for luncheon. Kildonan proposed having cocoa, and we all hunted for sticks among the low brushwood by the river's bank. A fire was soon lit, and our cocoa proved excellent. A cup of it was given to the head man in charge of the baggage, whose pony had fallen under him crossing a stream, and was shivering with ague. Too soon was the order given "Prepare to mount," and we continued our way, sometimes along fields, but oftener on stony roads. To my regret, my old horse fell lame, and I discovered he had lost a shoe.

The sun was setting, and its fading glory tinted the hill above Antioch. The modern town appeared quite Eastern in its aspect, and had an imposing appearance, not the less so when the old Jew received us dressed in his picturesque costume, and bid us welcome once more to his home.

Early next morning we bid a final adieu to our hospitable host. It being Saturday, the service of the synagogue was being held in one of his rooms. I trust our early departure did not inconvenience the worshippers, who sat with open door, their attention divided between the reader and our party, who were fastening portmanteaus and fuming over the delay in bringing the ponies.

"Sabbath" is very strictly kept among the Jews of Antioch. When we returned on Friday evening from Suweidiyeh, our own servants had to light our lamps, and do other necessary housework, and Constantin had some fears that we should get no dinner; but these, happily, were not realised, for we had our usual abundant meal, and both our host and his young-looking wife joined us **at** it. The lady could speak nothing but Arabic, but she took a lively interest in our doings. She reigned supreme in the household, her two daughters-in-law being entirely under her control, and not being allowed to have any share even in the management of their own children. They were pretty young women, in spite of the disfigurement of the stiff wigs which they wore, having at their marriage to sacrifice all their own beautiful and abundant hair.

Clouds enveloped the surrounding mountains when we left Antioch, and several drops of rain looked so suspicious that we dreaded a shower; but the weather cleared, and except that the wind from the hills, newly covered with snow, was piercingly cold, the day was otherwise fine.

We halted for luncheon at the same old khan where we had stopped before, and Constantin told me the following legend about the lake: "Many years ago there was no lake there, but a prosperous village amid beautiful gardens. One day a weary beggar carrying a child approached the door of a house in the hamlet. He asked for alms, but the poor widow to whom the cottage belonged said she had no money, only a little flour. The beggar told her to make a cake, which she did, and it proved a very large one. Avarice entered her heart. 'I will keep this cake for myself,' she said, it will last many days.' So she turned the beggar and the child away from her door. Hardly had they left, when a little spring burst out in the widow's home, which gradually increased in extent, till it swallowed up the whole village, and the lake which is still there was thus formed."

"Such is the story of the lake," said Constantin, as he threw away the end of his cigarette; "at least, he says so," he added, looking at the gay cavass with a glance of supreme contempt.

As we ascended the defiles of Amanus, the road seemed long and weary, for hour after hour in a saddle, to those who for years have not crossed the pig's skin, is trying and fatiguing. Kiklonan and Susan went on in front, not having observed that we were detained by my wife's saddle not being properly girthed, and her stirrup-leather in the **wrong** buckle. The cavass was greatly dismayed when he discovered their absence, and galloped on in pursuit of them, leaving us in charge of Constantin. When we made up to them, we found the cavass impressing on them the risk they had encountered of capture by the brigands of Amanus, who **are not** to be trusted by stragglers.

As we passed through Beilan, from an archway in the narrow street, to our surprise, emerged M'Gregor, Kildonan's keeper. He was rejoiced to see his master, and informed us that the Commodore and Parker had had no sport, and that we were sure to overtake them, for they had just gone out.

Soon after we came up to the sportsmen. Certainly they had seen no bears, but they had passed through a most interesting country, and had found a Crusader's tomb. I asked the Commodore what sort of quarters he had in Beilan, and he replied, "Oh! very good, only if I dropped my hat it would disappear through one of the holes in the floor."

Parker's face and wrists bore marks that he had gone through lively encounters with the "creepers of the East." They both looked very well, however, and, as they were not going to be beat, they intended to start next day to some fresh ground in pursuit of bears, the native shikarree having assured them that "plenty to be got in new country." When I heard of these bears, I recalled a conversation I had in Cashmere with a native official. In reply to my question,

"What sort of man is the Maharajah of Cashmere?" he replied, "He very good man; *but* all men are liars!"

On leaving the Syrian Gates, small patches of snow were lying on the banks near the road. We gradually descended through the Beilan Pass to the plains. We could see the roadstead and the *Griffin*, lying apparently quiet beside a large paddle-steamer, but "distance lends enchantment to the view," as we discovered later. The sun had set, and a bitter cold wind was blowing from the sea as we crossed the marsh, and a most poisonous smell impregnated the air.

We rode to the Custom House, where one of those kindly consuls, to whom we have already referred, did all he could to help us, for we needed aid. A steamer was being laden, and the pier was crowded with Arabs carrying enormous weights and throwing them down, heedless whether any person was in the way of them or not. The waves dashed against the wooden piles, and with some difficulty we were almost thrown into a shore boat.

How thankful we were to find ourselves once more on board the *Griffin*, where we were most kindly welcomed by the Princess and her sister.

As the Alexandretta society was formed altogether of consuls and their families, the continual mention of Consul This and Consul That recalled to my memory an old Scotch maid of my mother's who never could master Italian during our long residence in Italy, and who always spoke of Monsieur La Croix, the then Consul of Nice, as " Mr. M'Craw the Counsel."

The Italian Consul got up a picnic to Beilan, to show off some of the beauties of the mountain scenery to the Princess and Miss Hare. Some of the officers of the *Coquette* joined them in this expedition, and through our glasses we watched the party assemble near the landing-place and ride away. The Commodore and Parker were expected back that afternoon, and had joined the picnic at Beilan. In due course they all returned, the ladies having enjoyed the trip very much.

The Commodore and Parker had preceded the others on their return. No bears had been seen or heard of. Parker came on board a ghastly object, his head bound up in a handkerchief, and very hazy in his intellect. The Commodore soon explained how he had got into such a condition.

They were racing their ponies home along the level, when heels over head went Parker's nag, and on to his head went the rider. He lay stunned and insensible for a minute or two; but the Commodore, with great presence of mind, got him up on his pony the minute he opened his eyes, feeling sure that, if he delayed, he might not be able to get him on board at all. The surgeon of the *Coquette*, on his return from the picnic-party, kindly came over to see the wounded man, and prescribed perfect rest and cold water, till he could decide whether there was concussion of the brain or not.

Parker, with untold obstinacy, would join the dinner-party, would drink claret when champagne was sternly refused him, and, finally, would not go to bed till his usual hour. However, he was all right in a few days, but his arm and side were black and blue and stiff for a long time. Moral: It is hard to knock out of time a hunting-man in good condition.

Our time for leaving Scandaroon had come. It must have been felt by most of us that we should never again visit these kindly consuls and their families.

The future of Scandaroon may be very prosperous, should the Euphrates Valley railway terminus be there; but money is required to make a harbour and drain the swamp. Turkey never will supply the necessary funds. Let us hope that some other nation may open out this hidden source of wealth, and that the abode of the croaking frog may be cultivated so that Alexandretta may be raised to a condition of healthy prosperity.

On the 25th of March, at six in the morning, we left Scandaroon. A heavy sea, without any wind, made the *Griffin* roll tremendously; but we staggered on against contrary wind and tide. Several battles at chess were fought under great difficulties in the deck saloon. Sometimes, at a most important event in the engagement, a violent lurch would send all the kings, queens, knights, and pawns rolling away in every direction, the tone of the "Oh!" uttered when such a calamity happened differing in cadence according as it was given by the winning or the losing combatant.

On the 27th we arrived at Port Saïd, the intention being to leave the yacht there and to go up the canal as far as Ismailia, and thence by rail to Cairo; but the authorities would not let us land, owing to the appearance of the plague at Bagdad, every vessel from the Syrian coast having to undergo three days' quarantine. An Egyptian soldier was sent on board to be our guard, and prevent all communication with the shore, our enforced seclusion beginning from the moment he joined the ship. So we "up anchor," and made for Alexandria, cruising along the flat, uninteresting coast, and soon getting into the brown water marking the proximity of the Nile.

In the early morning of the 28th of March, we were all on deck watching the entrance to Alexandria. The harbours are magnificent; but we had to drop anchor in the outer one, beside some other vessels, like ourselves, flying the yellow quarantine flag.

As our quarantine had two days to run, the authorities sent a steamer and a large barge to take us to the lazaretto; but the Commodore refused to go, and we remained among our own possessions in our comfortable floating home. A pleasant breeze blew during the day, and, what with books and letters (for here we got all the letters that we had missed since our cruise began), the time did not seem long. Our correspondence had been addressed to Corfu and other places we had never visited, and contained news of various events of more or less interest to us, which afforded us much amusement while imprisoned in quarantine.

Wednesday, the 30th of March, was our day of liberation; but, before being set free, we had to undergo fumigation. A boat came alongside with a batch of quarantine officials and their followers. Three large earthenware bowls, having been placed near the companion-ladder, were filled with a stinking concoction of sulphur and water, and were then gravely carried through every part of the ship, from the engine-room to the forecastle, after which the horrid mixture was sprinkled everywhere.

Our worthy Scotch captain's face was a picture when he saw his decks polluted by what he called the vagaries of "these heathens and Turks."

All the men were then assembled on deck, and, with their various pets under their arms, marched past a bowl of burning sulphur. The Princess and the ladies refusing to submit to this process, a compromise was made by carrying the bowls past them.

After this abominable farce, we were pronounced "safe," and the quarantine was over, strict injunctions being given that all clothing that had been worn was to be dipped in the sea; but I am not aware that this order was complied with. For fumigating the yacht and crew, together with the cost of bringing the steamer and barge to take us to the lazaretto, which we did not use, the Commodore received a bill for fifteen pounds, which he declined paying, but eventually had to do so.

CHAPTER V.

THE PYRAMIDS

CAIRO—SHEPHEARD'S HOTEL—EASTERN SCENES—CAIRO BECOMING GALLI-CISED—VIEW FROM THE PLATFORM OF THE CITADEL—HELIOPOLIS—ANCIENT OBELISK—OSTRICH FARM—THE VIRGIN'S TREE—THE MU-SEUM—THE NILE—ROAD TO THE PYRAMIDS—THE PYRAMIDS—TEMPLE OF THE SPHINX—EXPLORATION OF A PYRAMID—VILLAGE OF GHIZEH—EGYPTIAN SOLDIERS.

CHAPTER V.

IN the afternoon we steamed into the grand
harbour of Alexandria, and landed at the
Custom House, where carriages awaited us, and
we drove to the railway-station, which we left at
six in the afternoon, arriving at Cairo at ten at
night. We took up our quarters at Shepherd's
Hotel, the half-way house of many Indian travellers on their way either to or from Europe, and
also the starting-point of many for the Holy
Land. We found it a most comfortable residence
for the fortnight we passed there.

It is built in two stories on four sides of an
inner court, and a broad corridor runs right
round the square, rooms opening off each side of
the passage. During the winter, the apartments
to the south occupy the best situation; but, when

we were there in April, they were too hot. The thermometer in our room was constantly at 85°, and that with windows closed and curtains carefully drawn in the early morning, according to the most approved Indian fashion. The broad verandah in front of the hotel is full of arm-chairs, occupied by men and women in varied costumes.

The pith helmet and bronzed complexion, together with an erect and soldier-like appearance, betoken the officer of India's irregular cavalry, ready for any required work, but equally pleased enjoying a cigar while seated in a comfortable arm-chair. The fair boy fresh from England, full of excitement and wasting his energy in riding donkeys in the hottest part of the day, affords a remarkable contrast to him. Many of the ladies, who were of all kinds, were evidently visitors to the East for health, the languid, drooping figure and frequent cough showing that they had been compelled to avail themselves of the last resource open to them. Others again, radiant in health and happiness, were touring for pleasure's sake. Then we were not without a "happy couple," whose distinctive mark was that they always came into a room and left it **arm in arm**.

We were such a large **party** that **at** the *table-d'hôte* we had a table to ourselves, and so had not the opportunities we should otherwise have had of making acquaintances among the old residents in the hotel. Many of the people who were still left had spent the whole winter at Cairo; others had been up the Nile, and were resting for awhile before taking flight to more temperate regions.

The part of Cairo where the hotel is situated is completely French, and quite new. To get to the Eastern part of the town the bazaar must be visited, and there from Europe you **step** into Asia. These narrow streets of shops **are truly** Oriental. The water-carrier goes past crying, "Come buy from me the purest nectar!" The sellers of flowers hold towards you the loveliest of roses, saying, "Pink and rosy like the setting sun." Riders on wonderful asses nearly run over you, and the veiled women, dressed in the long robes which stick out over their donkey's hind quarters, turn towards you those beautiful eyes which make you speculate on the features concealed by the veil. Fierce-looking men, armed to the teeth, swagger past. It is an extraordinary sight, and reminds one of a well-got-up fancy ball.

Cairo is full of antiquities, though it is becoming quickly a French town. There are many drives and rides in the neighbourhood, and much money is spent in building new houses and making modern squares. Many of the ancient mosques are tumbling to decay, and the beautiful tombs of former rulers are shamefully neglected.

One afternoon we went over a road composed of deep sand to the tombs of the Khaliffs, situated on the border of the desert. They are fine even in their ruin, and must have been magnificent when first erected.

One of the noblest of these relics is the tomb of Sultan Berkook, who died A.D. 1398. Part of the interior of the building is used as a mosque. It is wonderful how well the wooden lattice-work is still preserved; at least, our dragoman assured us that it was as old as the rest of the building.

The lattice-work in Cairo is very beautiful in the narrow streets of bazaars. While seemingly a never-ending bargain was being carried on, I used to interest myself looking up at the rare windows of curious carving, behind which doubtless beautiful eyes were watching my companion's attempts at getting things for a fair price. Some of our party purchased screens and other things made of these old Arabian carvings; but the shopkeepers cannot be called a very honest set of men, and always ask four times more than they expect to receive.

By another deep and sandy road we proceeded to the citadel built by Saladin A.D. 1166. We entered by one of the gateways called "Bab-el-azab." In the narrow place beyond the entrance the Memlooks were massacred by Mehemet Ali A.D. 1811. Farther, on the platform of the citadel, we saw where the one warrior who escaped saved his life by jumping his horse over the parapet, a fearful drop. The gallant steed was killed, but the man reaped the reward of his daring venture.

The mosque of Mohammed Ali is built on the site of Joseph's Hall and the palace of Saladin. The view from the platform on the south side of the mosque is quite magnificent, especially in the evening, which is the best time to visit it. In the far distance appeared the pyramids, with a background of the glorious Eastern sunset. Beneath us lay Cairo, with its white mosques and busy streets. The hum of the distant wayfarers rose up to us, borne on the soft northern breeze; and above us the dark blue sky, with its golden fringe, the light of the setting sun. It was difficult to tear Susan away from this entrancing view; but time and *table-d'hôte* wait for no man.

Another day we drove to Heliopolis. The road passes at first through a line of European-looking houses, and soon after we came to an avenue of trees. The way is well watered, and skirts bazaars, barracks, and palaces. After several miles we reached the village of Mataruyeh, through which we continued our drive for a short distance, and finally came to our destination, the obelisk and the site of Heliopolis.

Heliopolis was the most learned city of Egypt, corresponding to our university towns of the present day. Moses studied here, and Joseph married the daughter of a priest of the temple of the sun, called On in Scripture, which once stood here. The obelisk is said to be the oldest in Egypt. The name in the inscription is "Osirtasen I., who was the second king of the Twelfth

Dynasty." The inscription records the erection of the obelisk, and has been deciphered **by Dr. Brugsh Bey.** The obelisk is about sixty-two feet high, and is in wonderful preservation, only some beetle has filled the various figures in the inscription with mud. The following is what has been deciphered:

"The Hor of the Sun
  The life for those who are born
  The king of the upper and lower land
    Kheper-ka-ra.
  The Lord of the Double Crown
  The life of those who are born
  The son of the sun-god, Ra
    Osirtasen,
  The friend of the spirits of On,
    Ever living
    The golden Hor
  The life of those who are born
    The good god
    Kheper-ka-ra
  Has executed this work
  In the beginning of the thirty years' cycle
  He the dispenser of life for evermore."*

We passed some time in this most interesting place, but at length were fairly driven away by the numbers of children, whose continual cry for

* Vide MURRAY's "Egypt."

"backsheesh" was most distracting. They pursued us even after we were in the carriage, and the road was so rough we could not escape from them. Suddenly the coachman pulled up his horses and jumped down. Our tormentors fled *en masse*, while our defender threw clods of earth at them.

From the old-world scenes we drove to new. Not far from Heliopolis is an ostrich farm, which at the time of our visit had only been established for eighteen months by a French company. Leaving our carriage, we struggled on foot for some way along a deep sandy road, when we came to a gate. This was opened by a smiling native, who welcomed us with great effusion, and led us to a cottage resembling an Indian bungalow. We were received by a nice-looking man, a Spaniard, who took us round to see the ostriches. He led us first to a large kind of loose box, fit to contain the winner of the Derby, and pointed to two little round balls like ostrich eggs on legs; these were young ostriches six weeks old. There were in other parts of the farm fifty older birds. The company began operations with only one cock and two hens. There have been no deaths among the birds. When we visited **the farm in** April there were three cock-birds. One with black legs, which came from Abyssinia, was considered very rare. Our guide informed us that there is a specimen of this ostrich in the British Museum (perhaps he meant the Zoo). The other two male ostriches came from Soudan. The hens lay sometimes twenty eggs, but do not sit. The whole of the birds, except the original lot, have been brought **to** life by artificial means. The first take of feathers would be in June **of** this year, 1881.

Our polite host informed us that the ostriches are very stupid birds, and do not recognise even their feeders. They eat green **food, and,** when that is scarce, they take from two **to three litres** of dry grain a day.

We went to the top of the house, the view from which was uncommon, **but hardly** pleasing. Situated on the border of the desert, nothing **is** to be seen beyond the farm but a wide vista of sand, while within the walls the ostriches are seen stalking about in their roomy compartments. **We** said adieu to the solitary man who had enjoyed showing us the farm, for he said he lived the life of a hermit, and saw no one but natives.

On regaining our carriage, we had not very far to drive to the "Virgin's Tree." In a garden near a well grows an old and venerable sycamore, surrounded by a wooden fence to prevent visitors from cutting the bark or otherwise defacing it. The tradition connected with this most ancient tree is that Joseph and Mary and the young child rested under its shade when they lived at Matarëëh for two years, at the time the holy family were in Egypt.

Matarëëh has been identified as On, or Heliopolis. It is more than probable that they passed this way, for it was then the direct road between Syria and Egypt. There is no reason why they should not have rested here near the well. Let us not quarrel with the fond belief of centuries.

In driving home along the Abassayeh road, the air was soft and balmy, and the perfume of orange blossoms came from the gardens in this evening hour.

Fashionable Cairo comes out at five o'clock to "eat the air;" the smart carriages have running footmen before the horses, and as they run they clear the way with their wands. The favourite drive is along the "Shoobra road," a long, shady avenue, the trees on each side of which were planted by Mahomed Ali, and the principal evening of the week for everyone to go there is Friday. The Pyramids can be plainly seen in the distance, but in flat Egypt they are a landmark from many points.

As we approached the town, we met many carriages, whose owners were enjoying the cool evening air. We were hurrying home to dress for a long and wearisome dinner in a close and airless room.

The museum is well worth a visit. There are valuable jewels torn from the tombs, mummies brought away from their resting-places, all most wonderful; but I was most interested in humbler objects—old chairs, old ropes, old cloth, more than two thousand years old, all of which had a strange fascination for me. From the museum there is a drive through shady avenues across the bridge over the Nile. How strange it was to find oneself on the banks of that river, whose name alone brought so vividly to our memory old tales of Bible history and modern travel! The Nile is a broad, muddy river, and, in spite of its associations, I must certainly call its banks hideous. From the river the road takes a circular course, and passes palaces of the Khedive and of the Khedive's mother, returning over the bridge past a large barracks.

Over this same bridge we drove early one morning, when going to visit the Pyramids. Our party consisted of the Commodore and self in one carriage, while my wife, Susan, and Miss Hare went in another. The air was cool, and we rattled along the road which has taken the place of the sandy path the sight-seers of former days used to follow; but these were the days when everyone rode donkeys, which are now comparatively little used, as there are few places where carriages cannot go. A long avenue of trees shades the way, and the fertile plains watered by the Nile, so green and pleasant to the eye, extend for miles in the distance. Groves of fine date palms are also to be seen in numbers, growing to a great height and size. The road to the Pyramids was finished when the Prince and Princess of Wales visited Cairo in 1868. It only took us one hour and a half to reach the pavilion which stands under the mighty pyramid of Gazeh, and where the Empress Eugénie rested and was entertained when she came to open the Suez Canal.

The Pyramids had become familiar to us from the first day we were in Cairo. We saw them in every drive we took and from every height we climbed, and even when we looked at them for the first time they were not strange to us; we seemed to have known them all our lives; and now, standing immediately under them, the same feeling **of** old acquaintance remained. They are most wonderful in their massive grandeur, and there is a mystery about **them** which is no less astonishing that the object of their erection is not fully determined. That these magnificent works of human hands should remain for centuries, and that no **one** can positively state why they are, is a proof of the vanity of all ambition. However, I leave others to debate what these solemn-looking monuments are, and proceed with our experiences in **our** visit.

The hot morning sun on that 8th **of** April was beating fiercely on their massive sides. The adventurous traveller, who was already on the summit, looked a very **mite** on the elevated perch where he stood. Arabs surrounded us, offering to take us to the top, or to conduct us into the interior, and lastly expressing their desire to run up and down again for a—consideration. We turned a deaf ear to all, and gave our first attention to the basket of refreshments, which contained a large block of ice. It was carried carefully up to the pavilion dining-room, and we went forth to explore.

The Commodore had been in Egypt before, and wherever he went he met friends among sheiks and donkey-boys. On this occasion, besides Abdul, the clever donkey-boy, who was always in attendance on him, we were joined by the sheik belonging to the village below the Pyramids, also an old acquaintance of the Commodore, and a most intelligent man, who had worked under Colonel H. Vyse when he was occupied with his explorations. We toiled through sand down a steep bank, till we came to a large excavation, with cells cut in the rock. On we struggled till we arrived at the temple of the Sphinx, as this wonderful ruin is called. Situated in a hollow, within ten minutes' walk of the Pyramids, its original object, like that of so many of the magnificent remains in the East, was evidently that of a sepulchre, all the ground round it being burrowed with tombs. We went down a sloping paved path into the temple, the aisles of which are still intact, and we marvelled as we looked at the huge blocks of granite that compose its walls, one of them measuring eighteen feet in length and seven in height. From this temple we toiled through the deep sand till we stood under the Sphinx, that wonderful monument of a long-past age, which will remain there for many a year yet to come, with its calm, mysterious countenance, baffling all investigations as to its origin. All that is now to be seen of the Sphinx is its head and shoulders and back; the rest is buried in the sand. Several times the figure and remains of buildings near it have been cleared, but no sooner is the tedious work over than the wind from the desert covers all with sand again. An altar was discovered between the paws, which shows that the Sphinx was an object of adoration, for the smoke of the sacrifice must have ascended to the nose of the mighty idol, a feature which now, alas! is gone. The Sphinx is hewn out of the natural rock, and some idea of its enormous size is suggested by the measurement of the face, which, from forehead to chin, is thirty feet long. Each one of our party was differently impressed by the Sphinx; my own feeling was that of astonishment that such a battered and frightful countenance could convey such an idea of grandeur.

Our guide having invited us to rest in his house, we descended the hill to the Arab village, and were most hospitably welcomed by the sheik, who gave us coffee, and told us that all he possessed was ours. *Pour passer le temps*, he opened a box and produced his wife's dresses and jewels. The former were too complicated for male comprehension, but the jewels were very curious. A necklace, composed of square and round pieces of solid gold, was a present for a queen. The sheik with great courtesy conducted us back to the pavilion near the Pyramids, the shaded room of which was most refreshing after exposure to the heat of the sun. In the luncheon-basket we found everything we could wish to eat, but the servant had forgotten to send anything stronger than soda-water to drink. We discovered that the juice of an orange squeezed into a tumbler

with iced soda-water is most invigorating.

Some of our party entered the Pyramid. I did not, but remained satisfied with looking at the grand pile of giant stones towering up against the dark blue sky. The explorers came back delighted with their adventures. Each of them had two guides told off **by** their sheik to look after them. They climbed up forty-five feet over some rough stones to the entrance **to** the **Pyramid**, and, looking in, saw a perfectly smooth and polished incline, going down to a small aperture. With boots on it was impossible to attempt walking down. One Arab put his hand under one arm **of** the adventurer, the other guide put his hand under the other, and so supported, guided, and held up, each one glisséd down the slope. My wife said that her heart failed her, and she wished she had not come, when she saw how small the hole was, and that she had to bend nearly double in order to get through it. Before her was pitch darkness, and a dread of suffocation possessed her. But once through the narrow entrance, all was right, for the ventilation is perfect throughout. The guides lit their candles and handed their charges up the very steep steps to the great gallery—another long, inclined slope of the slipperiest and most polished stone. As they pursued their way upwards, the guides loudly encouraged them in their broken English, constantly inquiring, "You pleased with me?—you like me?" At last they came to a short, narrow passage, which only lasted for a minute, and they emerged into the King's Chamber, a lofty, square room, and the principal apartment in the Pyramid. In it, at the upper end, is the sarcophagus, without a lid, and with no hieroglyphics or any writing that can throw light upon its use. When struck, it gives forth a fine sound, like that of a bell.

One of the guides offered for "one shilling" to burn a magnesium light, showing them a long piece of wire, and much vaunting the sight which should be disclosed to them. The bargain was struck; the wire was lighted, and a moment of brightness showed the wonderful stone roof, each stone fitting the other with marvellous exactness.

They retraced their steps, and branched off to the Queen's Chamber. The descent of the great gallery was even more difficult than the ascent. A guide went in front to check the too rapid steps of the explorer, and another behind acted as a drag. An **Arab,** throwing himself **on the** generosity of the sightseers, burnt another piece of magnesium wire, showing the full length **of** the gallery, one hundred and fifty-one feet, and its height, twenty-eight feet. There was great clamouring for "backsheesh" when they emerged into the light of day. There is a regular and high **charge** made for each man, which is paid **to** the sheik, **who is** responsible **for** conduct **and** civility. But, besides this, according **to the** fashion of the East, something more is expected. At last, everyone more or less satisfied, we bid adieu to the sheik, and drove homewards.

Our journey to Cairo was even cooler than in the very early morning, for a breeze was blowing **in** our faces. We passed the village of Geezeh, near which is a palace under the shade of trees. The village was once the summer retreat **of the** Memlooks; now there is a barracks, and some nice-looking young soldiers were lounging about.

CHAPTER VI.

EGYPTIAN ANTIQUITIES.

THE ISLAND OF RODA—THE NILOMETER—PALACE OF IBRAHIM PASHA—OLD CAIRO, OR BABYLON—MOSQUE OF AMER—TEST COLUMNS—SNIPE SHOOTING—LOADING EGYPTIAN DONKEYS—THE PYRAMIDS OF SAKKARAH—EXPLORATION OF THE SERAPEUM—THE TOMB OF TIH—EMPLOYMENT OF IDLE HOURS—THE BATHS OF HELICON—ARCHÆOLOGICAL DISCOVERIES.

CHAPTER VI

WE crossed the bridge over the Nile, and shortly afterwards drove up to the steps in front of Shepherd's Hotel, and found we **were** in time for the *table-d'hôte* breakfast at twelve **o'clock**. How easily one accommodates oneself to circumstances, however different from his usual routine! The rule **at** "Shepherd's" was coffee, tea, rolls, and butter **at** any hour between seven and ten; *déjeuner à la fourchette* at half-past twelve; dinner at half-past six. On board the *Griffin* we kept home hours, but here was a complete change; yet we all ate our dressed dishes and drank our claret at twelve in the day. This system **is** only adapted to warm countries, and would **be** impossible in country houses at home.

The sun was too powerful to permit us with

any comfort to make an expedition at any time, except early in the morning or in the afternoon.

A carriage was ordered at half-past four, and we started to visit the Island of Roda, which, however, was not an island when we went there, for the river Nile had almost deserted one side, so that it was again connected with the mainland, but at the time of the inundations the waters surround it. We passed through old Cairo, and, leaving our carriage, walked down a short, sandy road, and crossed the dried-up watercourse to the Island of Roda, where, according to the tradition of the place, Moses was found by Pharaoh's daughter. But the most interesting sight is the nilometer, used for measuring the height of the river Nile. Passing through a garden, we came to what seemed to be a deep, square well, in the middle of which is a pillar with cubic numbers on it.

The first nilometer at Roda was built A.D. 705. The rise of the Nile is of vast importance, and is proclaimed once every day when the inundation takes place. Twenty-four to twenty-six feet is the usual rise at Cairo.

The palace of Ibrahim Pasha, which is in the

garden of the nilometer, is deserted, and falling to decay. The dragoman informed us that it was haunted, and certainly it had all the appearance of a place with a dismal story attached to it.

On regaining our carriage, we drove to old Cairo, or Babylon, where there are many old Christian churches. We entered Sitt Miriam, which is upstairs in one of the towers in the Roman gateway of Babylon. These Coptic churches are very ancient, and most **of** them have traditions. We were shown, in the **Coptic** Cathedral, stone seats, **on** which they say that Joseph and Mary and Our Lord once rested. The altars, pulpits, and pictures are very old.

Leaving the Coptic part of old Cairo we proceeded to the Mosque **of** Amer, one of the most venerated by the Mahomedans, though now not used as a place of worship. The court is surrounded by columns, two of which, placed close together, are called "Test Columns," and anyone who can squeeze between them is sure of heaven (so said the dragoman). This mosque was founded by Amer, A.D. 643. There is a tradition that the downfall of Moslem power will take place when this mosque decays away.

We drove home through old Cairo, in which we had some curious experience of the narrow streets and horrid smells of Eastern cities. During our stay at Cairo, on more than one occasion the Commodore, accompanied by Kildonan and Parker, went out snipe-shooting. The heat was very great, but they brought back the largest bags that were made, and the snipe were a great addition to the *menu* of our table.

An expedition was next proposed to the Sakkarah Pyramids. I could not go, but my wife did, and I leave her to tell her own story.

Four of us settled one evening that an expedition to the Sakkarah Pyramids should no longer be delayed. Abdul, the Commodore's special donkey-boy, was summoned to attend and be consulted. Although called a "boy," Abdul was a man about thirty years old, and the owner of some very fine donkeys. He acted rather as dragoman than as donkey-driver to the Commodore, constantly going out with one of the carriages; and he made much better bargains in the bazaar than anyone else. He recommended an early start next morning, and proposed that we should go by train to Bedreshayn, take our donkeys with us there, and then ride on to the Pyramids, returning home by another route. It is a pleasure being able to settle "on a certain day we shall do so and so," without the home addition of "if it is fine."

Very cloudless the day broke. We were up betimes, and the little French-speaking waiter, exact to a minute, knocked at our door, with the breakfast-tray. We had two miles to drive to the Boolak Station across the Nile. We met the market-people coming in, driving their donkeys laden with garden produce. An Egyptian donkey carries a greater weight in proportion to its size than any other animal, a fact which I know from my own observation. The plan in loading, is to put on him a bulk greater than himself, and, when the load appears more than he can by any possibility carry, then the loader gets on the top of all, and the poor little beast is compelled to go on his way. Strings of camels we also met, but they will not submit to carry more than is good for them, so they fare better. The road from the Nile bridge to the station is pleasantly shaded by lebbeken-trees, and there were still pools of water here and there left by the inundations. A truck full of donkeys, saddled and bridled, was the first that we saw as we reached the station. Our journey by rail only lasted one hour. We travelled through a strip of flat, green country, past magnificent forests of date palms, with monotonous brown sand hills on either side. Susan, who had been in Egypt before, and was familiar with some of the Pyramids, pointed them out to us as we passed. First came the Pyramids of Geezah (already described), and then within a few miles of each other those of Abooseer, Dashoor, and the Sakkarah. There was no wind, but there was any amount of dust. We were glad to leave the hot carriage at Bedreshayn and get on our donkeys. Mine, "Dr. Kenealy," was a very fine animal, and the side-saddle was comfortable. From the very beginning our donkey-boys were threatened with severest pains and penalties if they touched our donkeys with their sticks, so we went along quite happily. Donkeys walk a very good pace if left to themselves, and not hit and prodded to go at a speed beyond their powers. For the first half mile we were on a raised roadway with steep banks. In the fields on each side was waving corn, but earlier in the year the river had been all over them. We passed through a grove of beautiful date palms, and paused before a mighty statue prone on its nose in a hole, the colossal statue of Rameses II. We were passing ancient Memphis. Some of us wished to stop and admire, but the sun was getting hotter and the Pyramids were not in sight, so we pushed on, across fertile plains and by more date plantations, till we reached the village of Mitrahenny, where the villagers were on the watch for travellers, with old rings and coins, tear-vases and mummies of the Ibis rifled from old tombs.

We entered on the deep sand of the desert, at a point where we had above us the curious Step Pyramid, which looks very battered. It is shaped like the others, only **it is** not so high, and the sides are made in a succession of steps. The track now turned away to the left, up a hill of sand. My donkey-boy worked on my feelings, by assuring me that " Dr. Kenealy " would have **no** drink all day if we went up there ; but, by going a little farther on the level, there was a pool of water, where he could slake his thirst, so I went on, and had the pleasure of seeing " the Doctor " walk into a pool. I toiled up the sandy hill for a short distance on foot, but I was very glad to get on my donkey again.

We were now fairly in the desert, out of sight of anything green, nothing to be seen but hills and waves of sand. The advanced party I found already alighted, and collected under the roof that was to shelter us during the heat of the day. It was literally a roof only; for we sat in a large, stone-floored room, open to the front, and one side to the desert, while, at the back and the other side, were rooms occupied by the owner, and doubtless intended for the accommodation of travellers. Monsieur Mariette, who principally discovered the wonders of the Sakkarah Necropolis, lived in this house while engaged in his work of excavation. The Pyramids of Sakhara are the most ancient monuments in the world. The north, south, and east Pyramids are the tombs of a long line of kings, and the museum at Cairo is enriched with the spoils taken from them.

On what is called the Sakkarah Plateau are eleven pyramids. The largest of them is the "Step Pyramid" I have already mentioned. They are all in various stages of ruin. Adventurous travellers, as a rule, are content with ascending the more lofty summit at Geezah. Our object was to explore the vast tomb called the "Serapeum," about five minutes from the house. There was once upon a time a temple here, but only sufficient remains have been found to prove there was such a building. The sun was very hot, and the sand felt burning through our boots, so that it was a relief to enter, by the gate at the end of the inclined plane, the dark, vaulted passages, built to hold the remains of the Sacred Bull, whose life was passed in splendour at the neighbouring city of Memphis, and who, at his death, was embalmed, and placed in the wonderful tomb in which we now were. Candles had been forgotten, and there was some delay while they were begged and borrowed.

Wide and high subterranean passages, branching in perplexing numbers in all directions, made us keep close together, and well within hearing of our guide's voice. On each side were the tombs — large chambers below the level of the surface, each containing a huge sarcophagus — empty, and with the lid pushed on one side. This particular part of the mausoleum, for it is only a part, goes back to five hundred years before Christ. When the vaults were first opened, the walls were covered with stone tablets, placed there by worshippers, generally bearing the name of the reigning king, so that there has been no difficulty in fixing the date. Most of these stones have been removed to the Louvre and Boolak Museum, but there are still some left.

From the depths of the earth we ascended into the fierce glare of the sun, from which we were protected by blue spectacles that were a great relief to our eyes. We walked through the red-hot sand to the tomb of "Tih," the outer part of which is in ruins, but the inner chambers are perfect. It is marvellous to see the painted illustrations on the walls as brilliant in colours as though ages had not passed since they were executed, representing the life of "Tih" and his family. His story is a simple one to read.

We see him on his farm among his labourers; out in a boat catching swarms of fish; in his poultry-yard with geese and birds innumerable, and shooting from a boat with a decoy bird. "Tih," the inscription at the entrance informs us, was a Priest of Memphis, who married a member of the royal family. He lived **"to** a prolonged old age."

We spent a long time in this old-world place, and then passed out again into the heat, and made the road as short as we could to our haven of rest, stopping, before we went in, to make the donkey-boys loosen the bridles, which, according to their cruel and senseless custom, were tied so tightly back that **the** donkeys stood with their mouths open. The worst case of bearing-rein in the Park could **not** be more distressing. **Most** unwillingly did they let the poor donkey's head free, assuring us that when they were tired it rested them. Mahommed and Abdul had unpacked the luncheon basket, and in spite of the heat we managed to eat, but the oranges were the best part of the entertainment. We had four hours of idleness before us, and our only book was "Murray's Egypt." We read, by turns, the history of the Pyramids and the tombs. Miss Hare sketched a pyramid; some of us slept an uneasy sleep on the hard stone floor, with the luncheon-basket for a pillow. The donkey-boys stretched themselves on the sand in any shade they could find, and slept too, while the donkeys seized the opportunity of their heads being free to roll about with their saddles on. Some of the more restless spirits of our party, defying sunstroke and heat, went forth to examine the "Step Pyramid," and so the long, hot hours of the day passed.

Four o'clock came, and we were all delighted to get once more on our donkeys, and turn our backs on the desert. Our road was the same as the one we had followed in the morning, but, when we got to the railway station, we passed it, and held on our way to the banks of the Nile. There we dismounted, and the donkeys were taken down a perpendicular path on the face of the steep cliff to the river, where they were hustled on board the boat we were to cross in. When we had followed the donkeys on board, the large sail was hoisted, and we were gently wafted over to the other side. The landing was easily effected, as the shore was flat. After a two or three miles' ride over a level, sandy plain, we were at the baths of Helwan, which are held in high reputation. The springs, which are sulphurous, are supposed to be the place where King Amenophis sent the "leprous and other careless persons, in order to separate them from the rest of the Egyptians." There is a very fine hotel here, where we dismounted.

A telegram had been sent from Cairo ordering dinner, so **we** were expected. The sun went down as we reached Helwan, but the heat was still intense. In the courtyard of the hotel not a leaf stirred, and the air was so still that we were almost breathless. We had a very good dinner. Owing to some mistake in the telegram, preparations had been made for ten people, and, as we were only five, everything was **on a** most abundant scale. We had not very long to eat it, as we had a train to think of, and the station is ten minutes' walk from the hotel. Some of us rode, the others walked. We found all the first-class carriages occupied, so we preferred getting in all together into a second-class compartment, which much disturbed the station authorities. I believe, if they had had time, they would have compelled us to travel in the class our tickets entitled us to. Our journey was short, only fifteen miles, but it took us about an hour. In the clear night we could plainly distinguish the quarries of Toora and Masarah, which for four thousand years have supplied stones for the great cities of Egypt. I think nothing is more striking in Egypt than its age. We are accustomed to think of ourselves as a nation with a pedigree, but we are new and modern, with our many centuries of history, when we come to Egypt with its antiquity.

We reached Cairo by the station below the citadel, and found carriages waiting. We drove to Shepherd's Hotel, where we heard it had been the hottest day of the season, the thermometer on the verandah in the shade having been considerably over 90°

Since writing the above, I find the following interesting information in the *Edinburgh Courant*, August 5th, 1881:—

"Writing from Cairo on the 24th July, the *Times* correspondent says: 'The saying that it never rains but it pours may be now fairly applied to archæological discoveries. Long before the *savants* have had time to peruse, ponder over, or profit by the wonders recently unearthed at Sakkarah, they are now suddenly overwhelmed with a fresh supply of material in the form of the largest papyri yet known, and by the apparition of the mummies, with all their mortuary appendages and inscriptions, of no less than thirty royal personages. This discovery, which has just been made, calls for special interest in England, for among the thirty royal mummies are to be found those of King Thutmes III. and King Ramses II., the former of whom ordered the construction of the obelisk which now stands on the Thames Embankment; and it was the latter who, two hundred and seventy years afterwards, caused his own official titles and honours to be inscribed upon the faces beside those of Thutmes III. These two monarchs now lie side by side in the Boolak Museum, and even the flowers and garlands which were placed in their coffins may be to-day seen encircling the masks which cover the faces of the deceased, just as they were left by the mourners over three thousand years ago.'"

CHAPTER VII.

VISIT TO THE HOLY LAND.

A JOURNEY TO SYRIA—PROPOSED MODE OF TRAVELLING—THE COMMISSIONER'S CAMP—IMPRESSION OF OUR PARTY—ANCHORED OFF JAFFA OR JOPPA—AN OLD SAILOR—HOWARD'S NOTES—IBRAHIM DOOBINEY, OUR DRAGOMAN—PARTING LOOK AT THE "CEDRENE"—A RAMBLE OF JOPPA—SCRIPTURE LOCALITIES—RAMLEH—TOMB OF THE MACCABEES—LATRON—IN JERUSALEM AT LAST.

CHAPTER VII.

WE had **all** along determined that, when in the East, we were to visit the Holy Land. Easter Sunday this year fell on the 17th of April, and we all wished, if possible, to **be in** Jerusalem on that day.

Shepherd's Hotel is haunted **by** dragomans looking out **for** travellers requiring their services in Palestine. Travelling there is expensive; two pounds a head **is** generally charged for **a** small party, a slight reduction being made for numbers. This charge includes tents, food, servants, horses, baggage animals, and, in short, every expense that may be incurred. The Commodore finally engaged a good-looking Copt as his dragoman. His testimonials were excellent, and **I** believe in every way he gave satisfaction.

We had reluctantly resolved to part company

during the ride through the Holy Land, as we did not wish to incur the fatigue of travelling the whole way from Jaffa to Beyrout on horseback. Our plan was to cruise along the Syrian coast, the Commodore having so kindly handed the yacht over to us, and to stop at any convenient port, and make excursions into the interior.

The Commodore's camp was pitched for inspection one day on a vacant plot of ground, and we all went over to look at it. There were two sleeping-tents, a drawing-room tent, and a kitchen one. "Bishai," the dragoman, had evidently done well, for the tents were new, and everything very nice.

The days were becoming hotter and hotter; everyone was leaving Cairo, so the Commodore and Princess assembled their party, and we all prepared to depart from the old Egyptian city.

At six p.m., April the 12th, we steamed away in the train for Alexandria, and that night we found ourselves once more in our comfortable cabin on board the *Griffin*.

The pleasure of returning was lessened by the dispersion of our party; Kildonan and Susan were about to leave us. The former was re-

turning home by Naples, while Susan intended proceeding all the way to Liverpool by sea.

The break-up of a party is always a source of regret, and particularly so **in** our case, for we had all been on the most friendly terms. We were quite sorry that unavoidable circumstances should take two of our number away. The next day, Susan went on shore, and then embarked on board the steamer which was to take her home. Kildonan, with some friends, returned to Cairo, while we who remained put to sea at six **p.m.**, on April the 13th.

There was a heavy sea outside the bar, and **we** pitched and rolled a great deal. The moon rose bright and clear, **but** the wind was dead ahead. I sat on deck smoking a cigar and watching the waves as they appeared to run past us in an endless race. Sometimes the moon was hid **behind** a cloud, and the ghost-like, troubled sea was dark and gloomy; then the moonlight burst forth again, and the white-crested water-spirits seemed to roll and tumble in an ecstasy of joy.

The next day the sun shone brightly on a very rough sea. The sailors said "there must have been a blow somewhere to make such a terrible jumble." We basked in the delightful heat, and read, and smoked, and ate, and talked all day. The sun set in a most glorious golden sky, some treacherous-looking clouds surrounding him. As the night wore on, the sea became wilder, and the wind increased every hour till the south-west breeze became half a gale of wind.

We cast anchor at seven in the morning on the 15th of March (Good Friday) off Jaffa. The roadstead is quite unprotected, and when the wind blows from the south-west the waves dash upon the shore in great surf rollers. A large shore-boat, with some six or eight men, had come off, bringing an agent from Mr. Howard, the tourists' friend, to see if we required anything. The Commodore's camp, as he reported, was pitched close to his hotel, and the dragoman was expecting the yacht. The boatmen strongly recommended our landing as soon as possible, as the surf always increases as the day wears on.

We had intended taking things easily, and landing in the afternoon, but when we heard that we might not get off later we decided to land with the others. Very hurriedly was our packing effected. It was surprising how few things were forgotten, as we found afterwards.

The roar of the surf on the shore was getting louder, and the big boat alongside was rising higher and sinking lower than it was pleasant to see when we stood ready for the "Now!" that made us spring from the rolling *Griffin* to the unsteady boat. The boatmen were accustomed **to** this wild sea. The great waves appeared very angry. Sometimes we were upon the summit of a rolling mountain, then down in the valley. No wave broke over us, so cleverly was the boat managed. I could not help thinking of an old sailor's advice **to** an aunt of mine. Sandy Coid was half smuggler, half fisherman, and lived on **the** sea-shore, near Port William, in Galloway. My aunt often went out in his boat for a sail in Glenluce Bay. Once it came on to blow a sudden gale, and one **of** the ladies got very frightened, and annoyed Sandy by many questions.

"Hey, Sandy, what shall I **do**, if we are upset?"

"Do, mem," quoth Sandy, fairly driven wild by her appeals. "Put yer heed doon under the water, and droon as fast as ye can, for I couldna help **ye**."

At length we got into the ruined harbour, safe and dry. Jaffa, once Joppa, was a most important port. It is one of the oldest towns in the world. In the Bible it is mentioned as marking the borders of the tribe of Dan,* and it became the Port of Jerusalem. To it was conveyed the timber from Lebanon for the construction of both first and second temple.† Jonah sailed from it. ‡ St. Peter came from Lydda to Joppa, and raised Tabitha from the dead. There also was the house of Simon the tanner, "which was by the sea-side," and in which he saw the vision that showed him the future extent of Christianity.§

We landed among a crowd of dragomans and natives, and with difficulty scrambled along the ill-paved streets till we arrived at Howard's Hotel, situated near the sea, from which it is divided by an Arab cemetery. The day being Friday, the tombs were surrounded by women in many-coloured dresses, forming a *coup d'œil* of light and shade.

The Commodore, Princess, Miss Hare, and Parker were to part from us here for one month. The Commodore had, with the greatest kindness,

* Josh. xix, 46. † 2nd Chron. ii, 14 ; Ezra ii, 7. ‡ Jonah i, 3.
§ Acts ix, 36 ; x, 1—7.

told us that we might take the yacht anywhere we pleased, only trysting us to meet him at Beyrout on the 15th of May. We took up our quarters at Howard's Hotel, while the Princess and her followers went to their camp, which was pitched close to our garden. It was with a pang of real regret that we waved adieu to the camp party as it rode past the balcony, from which we watched their start.

As we looked beyond the Arab cemetery to the sea, we were distressed to see the *Griffon* pitching and tossing at anchor, and we were informed that no communication could be held with her till the sea went down. We dined at the *table-d'hôte*, at which there were only three other guests; the season was not a good one, the alarm of plague having deterred many from coming to Palestine. We soon retired to our rooms, as we were to make an early start.

On landing from the yacht we had been besieged by dragomans, anxious to be engaged, but we decided on making an arrangement with Mr. Howard, who has for many years acted as conductor, adviser, and manager to many of the hundred pilgrims to the Holy Land. We found that Mr. Howard's terms were most liberal and satisfactory. Before dinner, he asked us to go out and see the carriage he intended us to travel in. It was a small but comfortable vehicle, with a roof on four poles, and leather curtains. In attendance was a little, active man, whom Mr. Howard introduced to us as Ibrahim Dehrony, a dragoman. As we became quite attached to this man, I may as well describe him here. He was a Latin Christian, little and active, dressed, I must own, in a very peculiar costume. His head was generally wrapped up in a kefiah, or shawl; "for de travel," at other times he wore the Turkish fez. The kefiah was put on so as to cover his whole head, neck, and shoulders, and gave his intelligent face a fierce and rather savage look, for his moustaches stuck out with a defiant curl, and he had a large scar on his forehead, the mark of a pistol wound. His coat was a kind of drab overcoat, and his trousers were loose. On foot he looked like a fly; on horseback he was a warrior of the desert, with a perfect seat and very light hand. I never met a more attentive man, or one who had a better knowledge of the country. Add to all this, thorough honesty, and you have Ibrahim Dehrony, our dragoman.

At seven o'clock on the morning of the 16th **of** April, we were ready to start. Before leaving, **I** took a parting look at the *Griffin* from our balcony. She was plunging **in** the waves, and rolling fearfully. Through my glass, I saw no one **on** deck, and could **well** believe what discomfort all **on** board were enduring. The wind was blowing **full on** shore, and the waves were tumbling in a high wall of surf.

Our baggage was declared too heavy **for the** springs of our carriage, so we left it to follow on a mule. The distance to Jerusalem being forty-**two** miles, we were assured **it** would reach us the same night, but it did not, though the mule arrived at break of day next morning.

We rattled along the ancient streets **of** Joppa till we came to the new road, which passes through orchards of orange-trees, whose boughs were laden with fruit. The oranges of Jaffa are famed for their size, being enormously large, but not such a delicate fruit as the Maltese or Sicilian.

We enjoyed the cool morning air. Ibrahim called our attention to **a** strongly-built house near a garden, which is named "Tabitha's House." A road branching to the left leads to Lydda, from which St. Peter came when summoned to Tabitha's aid. We kept straight on, and passed on our right the plain where Samson tied the "foxes' tails." A little farther on was "Beth Dagon," the House of Dagon. On our left we could see in the distance Lydda. We were traversing the "Plain of Sharon," and in a short time trotted into Ramleh, nine miles distant from Joppa. Ramleh has been the scene of many battles between the Crusaders and the Moslems, and its ruined buildings testify to its former grandeur. It has generally been considered the first halting-place for camping parties, so we were not surprised to hear that the Commodore had pitched his tents there the night before, but they had started from Ramleh before we arrived.

It is singular how little is known at Cairo, by travellers, of the facility of reaching Jerusalem from Jaffa. Of course, it is the interest of the dragomans to ignore the possibility of driving in a comfortable carriage, for then the tents, horses, and equipage would not be required, and two days' journey becomes the affair of a day. When we were at Cairo, we could get no certain information on the subject. We were told that there was no public conveyance, no carriages between Jaffa and Jerusalem, and that the road was infamously bad. It was only on our arrival at Jaffa, when Mr. Howard's agent came off and gave us all details, that we ascertained the road was practicable all the way for wheels. A lady at Cairo was most anxious to go to Jerusalem, but told me she could not stand the fatigue of riding.

"Oh, if there were carriages, I would not hesitate," she said, "but my dragoman tells me there are none."

Our strong little horses trotted merrily along till we came to the village of Kubab, which is surrounded by olive groves. Here we drove down a steep declivity into a valley called Merj Ibriomeir—the valley of Ascalon. Having crossed this valley, we ascended a hill, and observed to our right a lonely house, with the sign "Howard's Hotel." Here we were to halt, in order to rest the horses after a twenty mile drive. Our carriage drove up to its door, and the solitary waiter was so much occupied hoisting the British flag in honour of our approach that he was not present at the door to welcome us. However, after having managed to get the flag half-mast high in a disordered kind of condition, he hurried down and gracefully ushered us into a comfortable room, where in due time we were served with omelette, beef stew, and potatoes for luncheon. While it was getting ready, Ibrahim requested us to follow him downstairs and out into the open. He led us to what appeared to be a well. Down a ladder he asked us to go, and when we had both descended into a subterranean chamber, he said, in solemn tones,

" Here, Milady and General, is the tomb of the Maccabees. It was discovered only a few years."

The vault is in a rock, and several empty niches round prove that it was used as a tomb.

Near the hotel is a village called Latron, where, tradition states, the repentant thief on the cross was born.

At luncheon the solitary waiter, glad to hear the sound of his own voice, informed us that his life was dreadfully *triste*. He was alone for days —he saw no one but the cook ; then came a rush of visitors. Last week Prince Rudolph of Austria, with thirty followers, arrived. He was the **only** waiter. He had so much to do that he got a *coup de sang*. The poor man looked ill.

"I am not afraid—no," he said, "but the evil people in the neighbourhood steal my fowls. I have sent in my resignation."

We said good-bye to this unhappy being.

The two hours' rest the Italian coachman had required for **his** horses having passed, **they** seemed quite refreshed, and started gamely **on** the worst half of the journey. A couple of miles after leaving the hotel, we entered the valley **of** Wady Aly. The terraced slopes of the mountains of Judah rose on each side of **us**. For several miles we toiled up the glen, recalling the Highlands of Scotland to our memory. It is not so long ago since this part of the journey was a terror to travellers, but now the road is considered safe, though here, as everywhere else in Syria, every man carries his matchlock, and often, in addition to that, a pistol and long knife. From here we descend through olive groves to Kerjath-jearim. This village has some fine houses, once the property of a great robber chief, Abu-ghash, who was defeated by Ibrahim Pasha, and hanged, but his body reposes in a grand mausoleum near the scene of his atrocities.

Our Ibrahim made us alight and visit a partially restored Gothic church of the Crusade period, which is very massive. "The ark rested in the house of Abinadab, on the hill," on the ridge above the village. The road which we passed along to Jerusalem was the same track by which David travelled.

The sky had gradually become darker and darker, and the clouds were hurrying from the sea to the mountains. We had now reached the highest point in our journey. The wind still blew fiercely from the south-west; the rain came down in torrents, but all we could do was to close the curtains of our little carriage amid exclamations of regret. We remembered at the same time, with anxiety, that it was the worst point in the compass for a vessel anchored off Jaffa.

It was eight o'clock in the evening, and quite dark when we stopped at the Damascus Gate of Jerusalem. There we had to alight, for no carriages can pass through the streets. In a downpour of rain, we stumbled and slipped along the ill-paved and ill-lighted way till we arrived at the Damascus Hotel. The sweet remembrance came over us, in spite of stones, and dirt, and rain, "At last we are in Jerusalem!"

Up a narrow stone stair, we followed Ibrahim to a paved court, open to the weather, with windows all round it; up another flight of stairs to an irregular court, part of it surrounded by the house, the other part overlooking the street below and the country beyond. Our guide opened a door, struck a light, and we found we had reached our rooms. I think a laundry at home would give the best idea of their bareness. The walls were white-washed, as was also the ceiling; the floor was stone, and the actual necessaries of life were there, but nothing more. A small, deep window looked into the courtyard, another one, so high up that, even standing on a chair, I could not reach it, looked in another direction, and there was a feeling of dampness in everything. Only the bed-room door separated us from the dripping courtyard and the pouring rain. Armed with umbrellas, we made a dash across to the *table-d'hôte* room, and that first night we dined alone. We were too late to get anything hot to eat, and too early for the food to be quite cold.

After a day or two at the hotel, we moved up another flight of stairs to a most delightful habitation. We were quite at the top of the house, and our sitting-room and the bed-room beyond it were the only ones opening off the court. We were perched, as it were, on the summit of the hotel, and the view was most interesting, for immediately in front, and only divided from us by houses lower than ourselves, and by the Valley of Jehoshaphat, was the Mount of Olives. There it was, always before us: in the early morning, in the daytime, and at night—there was that mount; the same in shape as it was when our Lord came down that steep path which we could see quite plainly from where we were stationed.

CHAPTER VIII.

IN JERUSALEM.

THE STREETS OF JERUSALEM—PILGRIMS—ST STEPHEN'S GATE—GETHSEMANE—TRADITIONS AND PROPHECIES RELATING TO JERUSALEM—DAVID'S TOWER—A CELEBRATED HEBREW SCHOLAR—PHYLACTERIES—AN AMERICAN PARTY—THE MOUNT OF OLIVES—HOSPITAL OF ST. JOHN—CHURCH OF THE SEPULCHRE—TOMBS OF THE KINGS AND OF THE JUDGES—VALLEY OF JEHOSHAPHAT—CHURCH OF THE ASCENSION—TOMB OF DAVID.

CHAPTER VIII.

EASTER Sunday was ushered in by rain. We went to the Episcopalian church in the citadel, near David's Tower. It was about ten minutes' walk from our hotel. The streets of Jerusalem are very badly paved with round stones, polished, not worn by the weather and traffic, and laid together with a small well of mud between each one. This gives some faint idea of what our difficulties were when we attempted walking. Riding was even worse; there is no foothold for a horse, and it was distressing to see the laden animals struggling along, slipping and stumbling. Part of our way was up Christian Street. We got to know it very well before we left Jerusalem, with its many shops of olive wood. Then we passed along a line of covered bazaars, and so up to the church. The streets were thronged with pilgrims, but a way was instantly made for us, as our imperious dragoman elbowed his way along through the crowd.

In the afternoon, when the rain ceased and the sun shone out, we went along the Via Dolorosa to Stephen's Gate, and, descending the steep path, crossed the Brook Kidron and came to Gethsemane. It is a sweet, sad place at the sunset time. The venerable olive-trees carry one's thoughts into far-back ages, and everyone must be impressed when lingering in this garden full of tender reminiscences.

While of course there is a great deal of reality, there is also a vast amount of fable about Jerusalem. But there can be no doubt that somewhere near here our Lord often went, so every spot is holy in spite of man's inventions.

On that Easter evening there was something very soothing in our visit to Gethsemane. The rain which had fallen in the morning had passed away, and the colouring of the heavens was very pleasing to the eye. The walls of Jerusalem appeared rugged and forlorn, but the hills on which they are built were dotted here and there with bright spots. And how quiet was Gethsemane, with its venerable old trees and garden of flowers, so sad and so silent, and above all how solemn were its reminiscences contrasted with the clash of the Turkish band and the distant hum of modern Jerusalem.

We remained several days wandering about through the narrow streets or riding out into the neighbourhood, and never for one moment felt that disappointment which I have heard many people say they have experienced when in the Holy Land. No doubt the city is changed by sieges and earthquakes. The valleys are filled with the débris of ruined buildings. No doubt our Lord never trod the Via Dolorosa, and many other places have been associated with reminiscences of his life which have no claim to such distinction, but there is quite enough left to increase our faith in all that is past, not only as regards the accuracy of the prophecies concerning this city which have been already accomplished, but also of what is yet to come. So I do not intend to question the truth of any of their traditions. Suffice it for me to mention and briefly describe the places that were shown to us, satisfied that the mountains and hills are the same as when our Lord lived and suffered in Jerusalem.

Ibrahim was always in attendance, ready to accompany us on our expeditions; indeed we could not find our way alone, for the streets are difficult to understand, they are all so like each other. We visited David's Tower. The enormous blocks of stone of which it is built are proof positive of its antiquity. It is easy to see the difference between the ancient and more modern masonry. At the entrance to the tower a guard of Turkish soldiers were lounging about, but they did not stop us, and we went up the steep stair till we got on the top of the tower. This tower has had various names; Josephus states that it was built by Herod the Great and called by him Hippicus, after a friend who was killed in battle. When Titus took Jerusalem he spared it. The historian of the Crusades, in writing of the citadel, names it the Tower of David, and it has remained till now much the same as it was in those days, having escaped destruction when the Moslems destroyed the city in the thirteenth century. On the top of the tower are placed small guns suitable for firing salutes. The view from its summit is very interesting. This tower is the commencement of the first wall or walls of Zion. We visited on our way home the shop of Shorpur, the well-known Hebrew scholar. He **has** a very interesting collection of old and rare manuscripts, and many other curious things connected with the Jews. He showed us two kinds of phylacteries worn by the Pharisees. Formerly nothing was more difficult than to get them, and Mr. Shorpur told us that long ago he gave thirteen pounds for a pair, but now he finds the Jews quite willing to part with them for a small sum.

The idea conveyed to my mind by the expression "making broad their phylacteries" was increasing the border of some upper garment, on which texts from Scripture were emblazoned. A phylactery is **a** small leather case (very like one of those square leather ink-bottles that cost a shilling each at home), containing verses from Deuteronomy, written on parchment; these are worn under the arm, pressed against the heart of the wearer, and kept in their places by long leather thongs. The ostentatious wearing of phylacteries consisted in doubling **or** trebling the size of the leather case, and in placing them above the forehead, where they **were** conspicuous **to** all beholders. Mr. Shorpur also produced an ancient parchment which was rolled up and fastened by many seals, all of which had to be broken before the parchment could be opened and read, making clear the meaning of the opening of the seals in Revelation. We bought some Bibles bound in olive wood, which he certified were made from trees that had grown on Mount Olivet.

When we got back to the hotel we found an American party at luncheon, whose acquaintance we made, and whom we met often afterwards. It is one of the pleasant features in a journey meeting agreeable people. There is a pleasure in comparing notes, and much information is gained if the people are intelligent and good-natured. We were particularly fortunate in our American acquaintances, whose usual residence was at Nice.

In the evening how delightful it was to sit out on our platform and see the Mount of Olives growing darker and darker, while the crash of the unmusical Turkish band, which always played at nine at night, reminded us that the Moslems rule in old Jerusalem!

Another day Ibrahim took us to the Hospital of St. John, near the Church of the Sepulchre. A magnificent gateway is the entrance to this palace of the Knights of St. John. It is in ruins, but grand in its decay. It was established in the eleventh century by the merchants of Naples. Two hospitals were formed, and were the origin of the Order of St. John of Jerusalem, once so powerful, now faded away.

And here we are in the cradle of this grand institution, among the fallen columns and noble galleries. All was silent where the mailed warrior had made these magnificent but now roofless halls re-echo with the sound of his voice and of his clattering sabre. From this monument of a noble order we crossed the narrow street to the Church of the Holy Sepulchre.

The Greek Easter Sunday was near, and the pilgrims crowded the Holy City, especially the neighbourhood of the sepulchre. Never before did I behold such a touching sight as the expression of faith in these poor people's faces. Most of them were Russians, and they came into the church with a look of joy. They knelt down and rose up, and knelt down again, and finally entered the chapel where they believed the tomb of our Lord is situated.

We went into different chapels sparkling with gems and gold and silver; but nothing seemed so real as the look of faith in these poor pilgrims' eyes.

We returned very often to the Church of the Sepulchre. In the court outside there are vendors of rosaries, made of shells from the Dead Sea, of beads and crosses from Bethlehem, and others of beads which have been to Mecca. These the faithful buy, and, after laying them on the sacred sites in the church, carry them home, to be treasured doubtless from generation to generation in the far away countries of Russia, in the islands of the seas, and in burning Egypt. For there are pilgrims from all lands. Ibrahim could tell us their nationality at once by some peculiarity in their dress. The Russians were always unmistakeable with their long, unkempt locks, the full skirts the men wore, and the heavy shoes they generally carried in their hands in the church. Some of these pilgrims, Ibrahim told us, had walked every foot of the way it was possible to walk, carrying with them bread sufficient to last them on their pilgrimage.

The Turkish soldier and Moslem peasant may

wander about unnoticed in the church, but the Jew is not allowed within the precincts. He may not come near the tomb of Christ.

In the afternoon we went for a ride. Ibrahim was very anxious that we should try the horses he had provided for our expedition to Jericho and the Dead Sea. My wife had a free-going young bay mare, which carried her very well. My Rosinante was not so young as he once had been, but he was very sure-footed, and awoke up sometimes from a ruminating study, when some fast-going mare passed him on the road. On these occasions he neighed ferociously, curved his neck, and made believe that he was a young and gallant Arab, like Ibrahim's nag. It was a pleasure to see our dragoman on any horse's back.

We went out by the Damascus Gate, and made for the tombs of the kings, situated about one mile and a half from the city. We got off our horses and descended a broad marble staircase of many steps, at the foot of which there is a wide, open area. On turning to the left, we passed into a large square excavation, out of which there is an entrance to a dark chamber, in which we lighted our candles and passed into the tomb of the kings. This vast place is also called the Tomb of Helena.

The cover of a sarcophagus taken from this tomb is in the Louvre. There is not much to be seen except the vacant niches all round, but the massive structure of a by-gone age fills one with wonder. We left the tombs by the same marble staircase, and, mounting our nags, proceeded to the tombs of the judges.

We rode along the Valley of Jehoshaphat. All the way is lined with tombs and caves in the rocks. The tombs of the judges are more ornamental than the others, having an architrave with flowers and tracery, but, alas! the entrance to the first chamber is very open, and goats and cattle have made it a stable, so that the state of the interior is not what it ought to be. Here, as in the other tombs, there are deep niches at regular intervals, in the various chambers opening out of one another. The earthen floor was slippery with dirt, and we were not sorry to leave it.

We remounted our nags, and, turning to the right, we went across country up the stony Valley of Jehoshaphat. It was a lovely spring day—all nature rejoiced to feel the warm sun after the late cold rain of last week. The country was green with young growing corn. Both riders and horses felt the exhilarating effect of warmth and sunshine. Ibrahim made his charger execute several manœuvres in a graceful and masterly way.

We now left the valley, and crossing the road to Nabulus, ascended along fields of young barley till we came to Mount Scopus, where Titus encamped when he attacked Jerusalem. The afternoon was far advanced, and the whole sky was softened by the setting sun. We rode to the highest heights above Jerusalem, whence, on our left, we could perceive the Dead Sea, and Jordan, guarded by the mountains of Moab, and on our right beautiful Jerusalem. **Yes**, I repeat, beautiful Jerusalem! At this evening hour the whole country round was bathed in the golden light of the setting sun. The clear air brought out mosque and temple, church and minaret, in the most softened colouring. The remembrance of our Lord's evening walks upon the Mount of Olives filled our minds. We were near the spot where He wept over Jerusalem. The sound of the Turkish bugles was borne on the breeze; the bells of the Christian churches pealed sadly; and the noise of distant traffic was distinctly heard.

Down the steep path we descended to Gethsemane, and then, ascending the other side, we rode round the walls of the city, till, by the Damascus gate, we regained our hotel.

On the Mount of Olives is the Church of the Ascension, a small chapel, quite bare inside. Ibrahim knelt reverently before the mark on the rock, which, according to tradition, is the print of our Lord's foot, as He ascended to the heavens; but the Bible says: "And He led them out so far as Bethany, and He lifted up his hands and blessed them. And it came to pass, while He blessed them, He was parted from them and carried into heaven." (Luke xxiv, 50-51.) The chapel is built in close proximity to a mosque. It is a Moslem who has the key of the Christian place of worship.

Near the top of the hill, not far from the other chapel, there is a convent, built a few years ago by a French princess, on the spot where it is supposed our Lord taught His disciples the Lord's Prayer. There is an open gallery, enclosing a court, reminding one of the Campo Santo in Italy. The Lord's Prayer is painted on these **walls** in every known language. The young Syrian nun who was showing us round the place next led us to **a** subterranean chamber **of** considerable extent, consisting of a broad, high passage, ending in what now is a small chapel. Here, as everywhere else at this Easter season, we found pilgrims on their knees. Our Lord is said to have instructed His disciples in this chamber.

We visited the Tomb of David. I have myself no doubt that this really is the tomb of the great king, and, I think, Scripture confirms it as being on Mount Zion.* Tradition says that David and Solomon were buried in the rock near the Cœnaculum. We ascended some steps, **and** were ushered into **a** passage. Through a trellised, wooden partition, **to** prevent the profane from pressing too near, we were told to look, and there we saw two large tombs, covered with a red and white drapery. The real sepulchres must be far below. This place is entirely in the hands of the Moslems, **and** they jealously guard it from the Christians.

* Acts ii. 29.

The "Cœnaculum" is under the same roof, and, doubtless, is above the vault where King David reposes. It is a large room, and for centuries it has been held to be the place where the disciples assembled at Pentecost, and where the sound like a mighty, rushing wind was heard, and this, too, is "the upper chamber" where it is said the Lord's Supper was instituted. It is a large room, fifty feet long by thirty. This also is in the hands of the Moslem.

During our stay at Jerusalem we frequently met the Commodore and his party. They arrived the same day as we did, having taken the usual two days to ride from Jaffa. Their camp was pitched in an orchard not far from the Damascus Gate. No better ground for camping could have been found in ordinary weather, but, alas! it was quite extraordinary. It poured steadily from Saturday afternoon, clearing for a few hours on Easter Sunday, and then coming down harder than ever on Monday. The tents did their duty gallantly for a long time, but the ground was getting hopelessly sloppy; and who that has tried it does not know the discomforts of tent life in bad weather? and, in addition to the rain, it was bitterly cold. My wife rode out on Monday to see how they were getting on in their camp, and found them just starting to take up their quarters at the Austrian hospice. A friend of the Commodore's had managed it for them, as this hospice is meant especially for Austrians. Jerusalem has several houses, built by the various foreign nations, to accommodate the pilgrims belonging to them. No charge is made, but it is expected that those who can afford it shall pay liberally for the hospitality accorded to them.

CHAPTER IX.

SCENES IN THE HOLY LAND.

PILGRIMAGE TO JERICHO—CAPTAIN OMAN AND THE "GRIFFIN"—THE TOMB OF ABSALOM—BETHANY—WILDERNESS OF JUDEA—A POLISHED STICK—PLAINS OF JORDAN AND THE DEAD SEA—WE MEET AGAIN OUR AMERICAN FRIENDS—WOMEN FROM A BEDOUIN CAMP—JERICHO—BANKS OF THE JORDAN—STORY OF A SPORTSMAN—THE TOMB OF MOSES—CONVENT OF MARSABA—WE PART WITH OUR ESCORT—AN OLD STORY—BETHLEHEM—TRADITIONS.

CHAPTER IX.

WHEN we went to our rooms that night, the 20th of April, we looked up at the starlit sky with greater anxiety than usual, for the next day we were going on our pilgrimage to Jericho. According to all ordinary rules, there ought to have been brilliant sunshine and no rain, so far on in April, but the weather in the Holy Land, as in other parts of the world, has changed, and Ibrahim would not go farther in his promises of a fine day than " in former years, it *will not have* rained."

So we rolled up our waterproofs, and I bought a pair of oilskin overalls in the bazaar, which I never had on, and we felt that we could defy the weather.

We were up betimes, and were much pleased to find that Captain Oman and the steward had arrived during the night. The worthy captain of the *Griffin* had a great wish to see Jerusalem, and now it was gratified. We heard from him that they had had a terrible time at their uneasy anchorage at Jaffa. For five days there was no possibility of communicating with the shore. Our old friend, H.M.S. *Coquette*, had passed on her way to Port Said, signalling that she had been ordered to Alexandria, where there was a row going on between the Jews and the Mahommedans, to quell which an English and a French man-of-war had been ordered up to see fair play. The Moslems asserted that the Jews had taken a Turkish boy at Christmas time and drained his blood to mix with their bread, afterwards throwing the lifeless body into the canal, whence it had been picked quite full of water! Proof positive of the crime. We had not much time to talk, as the horses were ready, and Ibrahim anxious for the start. But, on our return to the yacht, we heard what a perfect success the captain's expedition had turned out.

We left the hotel, promising to be back in three days. We pursued our way through the stony streets, our horses slipping and making a great clatter till we passed through the Damascus Gate, and, turning to our right, kept along the outside of the walls till we came to Stephen's Gate, where we descended the hill to Gethsemane, and continued on the low road to Bethany. This is the way our Lord came on His triumphal entry into Jerusalem. The road was thronged by Moslem pilgrims returning from Mount Nebo, where they had been on their yearly visit to the tomb of Moses. They carried enormous green flags and banners, and every now and then a gun was fired off. As we passed above Absolom's tomb, which is at some distance from the road, we saw an old woman throwing stones in that direction, and saying words we could not understand. Ibrahim told us that it was a ceremony she was performing, throwing stones and cursing Absolom's memory as a bad son. We met a continual stream of people. Whole families were out, the men on horseback, the ladies sometimes huddled together in a sort of palanquin fastened on a mule, and looking very uncomfortable and hot in their uneasy and cramped position. Then we met a gallant warrior in an eastern dress, who, we were informed by Ibrahim, was a "Knight of Jerusalem." "Is he a soldier?" I asked. "No, my general, a seller of cloth," said Ibrahim.

As we rode along this ancient road, suddenly Ibrahim turned his horse and said, "General, look!" And there was Zion clear and distinct in the morning light. The crowd of pilgrims pressing on towards Jerusalem were shouting to each other, and filling the air with sounds of exultation on their return from their pilgrimage to Mount Nebo. The congratulations of their friends who lined the banks, dressed in gay attire, made one think of the day when the Saviour came along this same road, riding on an ass, amid cries of "Hosannah to the Son of David."

It would have been a strange sight anywhere this multitude of rejoicing people, but here much more impressive from associations connected with the spot whereon we were standing, for it was the first glimpse of Jerusalem that anyone can behold coming from Bethany.

We turned our horses, and continued on our way. When we arrived at the village of Bethany, the first feeling was that of disappointment, for it is a very poor place, and very dirty. We left our horses at the entrance of the **hamlet,** and were conducted **to** a ruined house without a roof, not larger than a labourer's cottage. Here it is said lived Mary and Martha with Lazarus; and here, in two small rooms with ruined walls, our Lord dwelt when He visited Bethany. If this be not the house, yet it must be near the real abode of the sisters, and they must often have looked on the road beneath, which leads to Jerusalem.

The tomb from which Lazarus was raised from the dead is shown, but there are great doubts whether it is the real one or not. But, if not the actual place, it must be at **no** great distance from it, and the tradition which connects it with the two sisters and Lazarus is one which may well have been handed down from generation to generation.

The road after leaving Bethany was rocky and steep. The hills on each side were barren and rugged. The apparently endless cavalcades **of** Moslem pilgrims at last stopped when we reached, at the foot of a precipitous descent, an ancient well, round which were collected numbers of the faithful, their bright costumes relieving the dullness of the scene. Their road led them to the right, while ours lay to the left. We were now entered on the Wilderness of Judea, and it was, indeed, a dreary country, the white, desolate hills witnessing to the curse pronounced against it.

It is not considered safe to travel in this region unarmed. Ibrahim had a revolver fastened round his waist, I also carried one. Besides this precaution we were attended by a guard consisting of a sheik, the chief of a tribe, and two men.

The sheik was a most polished gentleman in his manners. When he first joined us he advanced with a most graceful bow, and kissed my hand, thereby swearing fealty to us. He was a very picturesque figure in his costume, and was armed to the teeth. He rode a handsome mare, that disturbed the usual placidity of my venerable Rosinante, and made him caper and squeal in a most irritating way, whenever he caught sight of her.

We continued our journey through the glen for some distance, and ascended a long hill, till we arrived at a ruined khan, in the most dangerous part of this wild country. It is here that the scene of the parable describing the traveller falling among thieves is laid. The sun had become very powerful, and the only shelter we had was in a cave not far from the road. Ibrahim had always looked forward to having this cave for our noonday's rest, and was quite distressed when he found it already occupied by a French lady and two gentlemen. We had to make the best of it, and take up our quarters at an angle of the rock which the sun was rapidly reaching. **We** had just time to eat the luncheon Ibrahim had provided, when the enemy was **on us,** and **we were** compelled to go forth in search of shade.

The blazing mid-day sun filled the whole land with light. **We** looked at the top of the **hill** above us, and, bringing our experience of Scotch hill-sides to bear on the present occasion, climbed up, making certain some overhanging crag would be found that would afford us shelter till the fierce glare of the next few hours were past. Vain hope. The higher we climbed the wider was the extent of sun-beaten country stretched before us. But so far our climb was rewarded, for we discovered below some ruined houses, close to the place where we had lunched.

Almost overcome by the heat we descended,

and, full of hope, turned to the ruins. The sun was so exactly above us that only one hand's breadth of shade could be obtained. Here we sat down, and I smoked, while Ibrahim, much disturbed by our discomfort, brought us some coffee to raise our spirits—but it was too hot to enjoy anything. As the slow hours passed, we had no amusement beyond that of watching the marks we had put to show when the shadows began to lengthen. My remembrance of the good Samaritan will always be associated with Khan-el-Ahmah.

Whenever we could, we got on our horses, which all this time had been standing with bridles tied to a stone, pictures of patient resignation, without food or water. The scenery, which was the wildest imaginable, soon disclosed to us the most magnificent ravine, several hundred feet deep, and very narrow. A little further on, and before us, were the plains of Jordan and the Dead Sea. Deep down in the ravine is the Brook Cherith, where Elijah was fed by ravens. As we rode past, numbers of black birds were soaring through the air.

The descent towards Jericho is very steep,

down the rocky, slippery road, and the heat was intense as we rode along the plain. We passed several large mounds, which have been opened by the English Exploration Society, but, as Ibrahim told us, they found nothing.

It was delightful **to** find ourselves once more in sight of anything green; the brushwood and trees showed that we were now near water, and soon our horses were knee-deep in a rushing brook, after crossing which we had only a little way to go, when we were on the site **of Old** Jericho. Our tents were pitched close to the clear stream—behind them rose the Hill **of** Quarantaina, the scene of our Lord's temptation, and not far off was the fountain, which once was bitter, and now is the sweetest water I ever drank. On a mound overlooking our camp were French and Austrian tents, their national flag flying above them, as our Union Jack did over us.

We were unpacking in our tent, when we heard a familiar voice saying, "There is a new camp since we went out this morning. English by the flag." So **we** knew our American friends from Jerusalem were also halting at Jericho. It was just the hour when people concluded a day's march. The next riders that appeared were the Commodore and Parker, who had already passed one night at Jericho, and now approached, followed closely by the ladies of their party, all very well mounted on showy little Arabs. They had gone in the early morning to the Dead Sea, and returned by the river Jordan, resting and bathing there.

Their camp was some ten minutes beyond ours, and, as we proposed turning in early, we saw no more of them that night. Our next visitors, the women from a Bedouin camp not very far off, came in the dark of the evening, when they appeared like ghostly figures in their dark blue robes. I rather mistrusted them, remembering the adventures of a lady who, during her travels in Palestine, had everything, even to her riding-habit, stolen out of her tent. Ibrahim assured me that he had not the least intention of sleeping, and our tent was well guarded. The sheik's sentries called out every now and then, and some one coughed at intervals, a forced cough, to show that he was there and awake all the night through. It was frightfully hot, not a breath of air to be had.

When three a.m. came, we were ready **to say,** "Ay, ay!" to Ibrahim's summons. We had decided to start early, dreading the heat of the Dead Sea, lying as it does thirteen hundred feet below the Mediterranean. We finished breakfast before the dawn had asserted itself; our tents were struck, and we were on our horses winding our way through the bushes of Old Jericho before the sun even peeped over the distant hills from which the Israelites looked down on the land flowing with milk and honey. The curse pronounced against Jericho is fully accomplished. No one would imagine that a great city once existed where now shrubs and a few mounds of earth mark the spot upon which it was built.

Half an hour's ride brought us to New Jericho, consisting of a few squalid huts, a Greek convent, white-washed and uninteresting in appearance, all that now mark the site of the place where our Lord came on His way to Jerusalem, and where He lodged with Zacchæus (Luke xix, 2). After leaving the fertile land watered by the stream passing Jericho, we came to a long, weary reach of sand. Before us in the distance was a line of green, marking the banks **of the** Jordan, but everywhere else nothing was to be seen but white, dazzling sand. How much more glaring it must be under the full power of the summer sun!

While we were contemplating the scene before us, Ibrahim pointed out a convent where a few monks of the Greek church strive to forget the world and to win heaven by a life of self-sacrifice.

We were now on the edge of the line of green that denoted the river, though it was still at some distance, "for the Jordan overflows his banks at the harvest season," and, wherever the water had been, brushwood had sprung up thick and dense.

The morning breeze was cool, and when we arrived at the banks of the river, sacred as the place where our Lord was baptised by John, the Jordan was flowing past, a rapid stream. Fine trees grow on its banks, and as we looked on this river, with which to every Christian so many interesting events are associated, one tree covered with flowers, being shaken by the breeze, anointed us with sweet-scented blossoms. Some of these shrubs may be the balsam which at one time grew here in great profusion.

After a short halt we had to bid adieu to the Jordan with all its memories. Before we left, we learned that wild boar and hyenas are found **occasionally in** the jungle near. A good story **is** told of a distinguished sportsman who, not long ago, killed many pigs when encamped at Jericho.

Being anxious to shoot a hyena, his attendants, to please their master, placed a dead cow filled with poison in **a** likely place for **the** stinking beast to come. The gallant sportsman proceeded to a concealed spot, there to await the hyena's approach. The day was hot, the stillness great; anyway, the watcher fell asleep, but awaking afterwards rode home without ever firing a shot. Having returned to his tent, he was surprised to hear a noise and shouting, and still more disgusted to see a dead hyena brought into camp, amid great demonstrations of joy, and laid down before his tent as **a** trophy **of** his good aim, when in reality he had never seen the beast, which had committed suicide by eating the poisoned cow!

The approach to the Dead Sea, which is among sandy hillocks, is dreary in the extreme. Fortunately for us, the fresh breeze that was blowing tempered the intense heat that has been so often described. Dull waves lapped the sandy beach, which was strewn with whitened branches that had been swept into the sea's horrid embrace by the river. We dipped our hands into the water, and then held them to our lips. The taste is horrible. We saw no birds skimming over the surface of the lake, and the hills around seemed powdered with sulphur. It is a dreadful place, and we had no wish to linger on its shore. My most anxious desire was, "Let us be gone at once."

We rode across the plain for about an hour, and passed many pools of brackish water, in which canes seemed to flourish. Then commenced the ascent of the mountain, by a steep, narrow path. The higher we went the more we could see of the Jordan, a green ribbon marking its way to the Dead Sea, which was dazzling in the sun. To our right, in the far distance, on the top of a hill, Ibrahim pointed out the highly venerated, so called Tomb of Moses, the object of Moslem adoration. We were now on the summit of the highest hill, and from it there is a fine view. We presently began descending a slippery path, over very rocky ground. My wife's mare had, heretofore, proved herself a most sensible and quiet animal, but, for some reason or other, she now began to kick viciously going down one of these steep descents. Her muleteer rushed forward to her help in time to prevent any catastrophe which might have happened on this dangerous road. My steed walked and slipped alternately in a resigned way. By the look of his ears, I gathered that he felt he had a certain way to go with a weight on his back, and he was blowed if he would go faster or slower for anyone. So I let him have his own way.

We had now been in our saddles for more than six hours, and, having only had a very light breakfast before leaving Jericho, we were quite ready for rest and food, "if" only a patch of shade could be found, or even a place where we might get a breath of air. Truly Judea is a shadeless, thirsty land. The only water we saw in the desolate, hilly region between the Jordan and the Convent of Marsaba was about half way. In a hollow below the path there was a small reservoir, covered with green scum. The muleteer let down a mug by a string, and drank some of it. I asked Ibrahim if it was good water. He replied,

"No, general. Too bad."

He carried two "gurglets" of drinking water for us, but it got tepid and undrinkable as the hours went by. At last, as there was evidently no shade to be found, we called a halt, and, endeavouring to shelter ourselves under umbrellas, had luncheon spread on a rock. I cannot say that we had much appetite, for the unfailing hard-boiled eggs and cold fowl, and lukewarm lemonade is not refreshing. There was no use attempting to rest, and, as our horses could get neither food nor water till their journey's end, it was better to push on.

In time we arrived at the valley below Marsaba, and then began our final ascent. On each side of the gorge rise high cliffs, and, near the top, the road appeared to have been more carefully made, at any rate it had been paved, and our horses slipped and stumbled along. Suddenly we came on the Convent of Marsaba, rising like a fortress before us, its lofty towers casting a broad shadow across our road. We had ridden the long march so quickly that the baggage animals had only arrived a short time before us, although they had come straight from Jericho, and had not diverged, like us, to Jordan or the Dead Sea. So our camp was not pitched. Till that was done, we bivouacked by the roadside, under the walls of the convent, for we could not go in, as no ladies are admitted. At last Ibrahim informed us that everything was ready, and we were not sorry to go to our tents.

Our camp was pitched in a gully, hills all round it. It had a picturesque effect, with the horses and mules picketed in rear. The wild figures of our armed followers contrasted with the peaceful character of the scene. The sheik occupied a prominent position on a crag, with his long gun like a field-piece at rest beside him. How thoroughly we enjoyed the ice-cold water from the depths of the convent well!

The Convent of Marsaba is built on a rock above the ravine of Kidron. It is quite a puzzle how so enormous a building could have been erected in such a place. The founder was St. Sabas, who was born A.D. 439, and died A.D. 532. With a letter of recommendation from the proper authority at Jerusalem the hospitality of the convent is extended to men, for, being a Greek convent, as I have already said, no ladies are permitted to enter its gates.

As it was a breathless night, my wife had untied the strings that fastened the walls to the roof of the tent, to try to get as much air as was possible; but we were suddenly awakened by a squall which had rushed down the gully, and finding our tent in its way, with full liberty to enter, was now committing wild havoc among our property. The roof was straining at the ropes, and we were within an ace of being left homeless and clothesless. The hubbub was tremendous.

Gallantly, Ibrahim, cook, waiter, sheik, escort, and muleteers had rushed to the rescue. Tent pegs were beaten down, and huge stones placed on the ropes to keep them steady—every loosened cord was tied again, and all missing property recovered. It was all over in a short time. The storm cooled the air, which was fresh and pleasant when we started on our homeward journey in the morning.

We had arranged to start at six a.m., so Ibrahim had us up very early. Here we parted with our guard, the sheik bidding us a friendly adieu, and not refusing the backsheesh I offered him.

At the commencement of our ride the road was very precipitous, and continued so for some time;

but at length we came upon fields of barley, fast ripening, near which were camped a tribe of Bedouins. These people, who are the real cultivators of the soil, seem to have no villages, but only camps. Their tents, which are low and black, are made of camel's hair. The first encampment we came to had evidently been settled there some time. Women and children were in and outside the tents, and the dogs flew out and barked at us, while some of the boys asked for backsheesh. Most of the men were out in the fields.

"Are they not great robbers, Ibrahim?" I asked.

"No, general," replied Ibrahim; "they very good men, they very *quite*" (quiet).

How old stories come back to me! Many years ago my regiment was quartered at Corfu. A detachment was at Vigo, and the orderly captain's duty was to turn out the guard at night and receive from the sergeant in charge a written report of absentees. To perform this duty he had to go in a boat. On "Patrick's day" the captain proceeded as usual to Vigo, and received the written report from the non-commissioned officer. Curious to know how many men were absent on this Irish festival, he examined the paper, and read, " etc., etc., etc., all drunk, but *quite*," which said as little for the sobriety of the detachment as for the spelling of the sergeant.

We came soon after to another Bedouin camp, which was in the process of being pitched. A difference of opinion evidently existed between the sheik of the tribe and a very randy-looking woman, for they were both speaking in the loudest tones. Of course we could not tell what they were saying or disputing about, and all Ibrahim said on the subject did not contain much information: " Ah! general, it is a *womans!*" We rode on through green fields, in which the fresh morning air was exhilarating. At length, at a turn in the road, high up on the mountain before us, appeared a line of light. As the sun shone forth, the line was clear and bright, but when the clouds darkened its rays, the line became dull and grey. This was Bethlehem. The approach to it is up a gradual ascent through olive-trees and vineyards. Before us was the scene where Ruth gleaned in the fields of Boaz (Ruth ii.), and where the shepherds kept their watch **by night,** and do so still.

We rode up **to** the convent door, and were admitted by an Italian monk, who took possession of us, and was very kind. First he showed **us** into the refectory, where luncheon was ordered, and then he took **us** to see the sacred sights. The way by which we were conducted led through what the monk called the Basilica, said to have been erected by Helena, and consequently very ancient. Several marble columns surround the court. But the Christian sects quarrel terribly, and the Armenians, Latins, and Greeks have each their different chapels.

Descending a stair, our attendant took us **to** St. Jerome's tomb, and then to his study. The chapel of the nativity **is** hewn **out** of the rock, and on a slab is written,

> Hic de Virgine Maria
> Jesus Christus natus est.

Near here, in this chapel, if not on this spot, our Saviour was born. The inventions to which one listens are distressing, and, like an untruthful acquaintance, annoy one continually; but as we turn with pleasure and confidence to a trusty friend, so the one fact is always a comfort—that our Lord Jesus Christ was born at Bethlehem.

We were taken to chapel after chapel, and were told many things. But the most interesting sight was the country round, the olive-trees, and the vines. Our Italian monk brought us back to the refectory, where we had luncheon, and he produced a bottle of wine called Bethlehem, made by the monks from the convent vineyards. At the hotel at Jerusalem we had tasted some horrid decoction going by that name, so it was with fear I drank some out of the monk's bottle, but it was excellent. As we left Bethlehem when the sun was very high there were not many people moving about the streets, but the men we observed were fine, handsome fellows, and the women lovely. We passed Rachel's tomb, of which there is no doubt, "And Rachel died and was buried on the way to Epratha, which is Bethlehem." We rode on past Mara Elias, a convent at the top of a hill, from which there is a view of Jerusalem on one side and of Bethlehem on the other. At the side of the road, Ibrahim pointed to a rock with an indentation in it about the size of a man, which tradition asserts was made by Elijah, who rested there and left that mark. We skirted well-cultivated fields **till** we arrived at a well. Again tradition states that the wise men, when sent away by Herod, came to this place, and, leaning down to draw up water, saw the star that **was to** guide them reflected in its depths.

As we approached nearer the city, we followed a road to the left, and, descending a steep hill, came to **a spot** where **Mr.** Cook **is** said **to be** going to build an hotel. A little farther on the Russian hospice is seen, and, following the track along the outside of the city walls, we arrived at the Damascus Gate, and at twelve o'clock on the **23rd** of April we were established once more in the hotel at Jerusalem.

CHAPTER X.

THE JEWS IN SYRIA.

MOSQUE ON THE SITE OF THE TEMPLE—THE MOSQUE OF AKSA—FOUNTAIN IN THE COURT—THE CRADLE OF JESUS—DESCENT OF THE HOLY FIRE—DEPARTURE FROM JERUSALEM—A SELF-WILLED OLD LADY—THE RUSSIAN HOSPICE—PILGRIMS—JEWS—THE JEWS' WAILING-PLACE—SMOKING IN THE EAST—IN THE "GRIFFIN" AGAIN—DEPARTURE FROM JOPPA—ST. JEAN D'ACRE—ANCHORED OFF HAIFA.

CHAPTER X.

NEXT day we attended the Episcopalian church near David's Tower. In the afternoon we got an order to visit the mosque built on the site of the temple. The first temple stood four hundred and twenty-three years, and was destroyed by Nebuchadnezzar. The second temple was begun B.C. 534, and, after suffering both from foreign invaders and **from** the Jews themselves, it was rebuilt by Herod the Great, but not completed for many years. The Jews spoke the truth when they said " forty and six years was this temple in building."

For the first week that we were in Jerusalem, the mosque was closed to all but the followers of the prophet, our Easter week being also a sacred time to the Moslems. It is not many years since permission has been given to the Christian to enter even the precincts of the mosque, but now-a-days an order from the consul of the nation to which the visitor belongs is sufficient. The consul sent his cavass as escort. Attended by him and a Turkish soldier, we entered the walls of the Haram by the Gate Babes Silsilah. We found ourselves in a long oblong enclosure, the eastern side measuring fifteen hundred and thirty feet, the southern nine hundred and twenty-two, the west and north sides being somewhat longer. The grass was green and untrampled, though many hundreds press it daily. The mosque itself stands nearly in the centre of the enclosure, on a raised platform of five hundred feet by four hundred and fifty. Crossing over the site of the Citadel of Antonia, of which there are no remains, we ascended the flight of steps to the higher ground on which the mosque stands. There is no doubt that the whole plan of the Temple of Solomon is changed. The site is the same, but beautiful as the mosque is, and extensive as the court outside may be, yet the splendour of the temple is no more, and there is the usual look of decay everywhere so characteristic of all that is Turkish.

We entered the "Kubbet-es-Sukrah," the Dome of the Rock. This beautiful building crowns the summit of Mount Moriah, and was built by Khalif Omar. It is octagonal in shape, and the walls are of marbles all different in colour. At some height are numerous windows of stained glass. Beautiful inscriptions in Arabic grace the walls. Four doors, facing north, south, east, and west, form the entrances. The dome is over the rock, which is protected by a rather high balustrade. So high is it, that I had to get on an elevated platform before I could see the whole of the rock, which looks rugged and unhewn beside the exquisitely-coloured marbles and the brilliantly-stained windows above it. The sheik of the mosque showed us round the building, and, having led us over the upper part, he conducted us to a cave immediately below the rock, and there pointed out the round hole which pierces the rock overhead, and through which he told us Mahomet ascended to heaven.

The floor of the cave sounded quite hollow. Every corner has its own tradition. If the Exploration Society were permitted to examine carefully underneath, they no doubt would discover much that is now hidden, and which would throw great light upon the history and structure of the temple. On again ascending to the mosque, the sheik took us to a slab of jaspar, and informed us that Mahomet had driven nineteen golden nails into it. One of these nails falls out at the end of an epoch. Three and a half nails are all that now remain, and when all are gone the knell of El-Islam and of the world will have sounded. From this place will be heard the trumpet blast announcing the Judgment. The sheik also told us that, if a silver coin was thrown by anyone and hit one of the nails, the thrower would assuredly go to heaven, which I suppose was a delicate way of hinting that a little backsheesh would be acceptable. Leaving the Mosque of the Rock, we crossed the area by the graceful little dome, where tradition says Solomon stood to pray when the temple was completed, and entered the Mosque of Aksa. This is a very grand building, "and has the form of a basilica of seven aisles. It is two hundred and seventy-two feet long, by a hundred and eighty-four feet wide, thus covering about fifty thousand square feet, or as much space as many of our cathedrals."* When we entered, several women were at their devotions.

On our way we passed the marble fountain called El Kar, "The Cup." Beneath this there is a subterranean reservoir, into which the water from the Pools of Solomon was once conveyed. It is nearly fifty feet deep, and interspersed with little islands of rock, upon which similar shaped tapering rock-work has been raised to support the ground above. When we visited it, numbers of the faithful were washing their feet in the fountain. In our rambles we saw several praying stations, on which were rows of Moslems kneeling. They reminded me of soldiers being exercised at "extensive motions," for, at a certain word or sign, the two kneeling ranks bowed their heads, touching the ground together, and springing up to the standing position, till the word was given, and down they went again.

South of Aksa there are some magnificent fragments of columns of verde antique and porphyry, on one of which, projecting from the wall above, the Moslems say that Mahomet will sit at

* Murray's "Hand-Book."

the day of judgment, and direct affairs in the valley beneath.

The sheik procured a key, and opened a door through which we descended by steps to a subterranean chamber, where we saw a sculptured sarcophagus called the Cradle of Jesus. By another flight of steps we went down to the vaults, the roof of which is supported on many columns. Each of these pillars has a hole in it, by which the crusaders fastened their horses, when these vaults were used as a stable. The place is lit high up at one end of it.

On leaving these vaults we walked round the area and examined the golden gate, now built up. The sheik told Ibrahim that by it a Christian warrior would enter Jerusalem and seize the city. Although we were in Jerusalem during the Greek Easter, we did not care to witness the strange scene of the "descent of the holy fire," which takes place in the Church of the Holy Sepulchre. Our friends were present, and described what they saw to us.

The ladies were high up in a gallery, in which there were seats only in front, already appropriated by first-comers. The men got places lower down, in what looked like the boxes at an opera, beside their consuls. The whole area of the church was thronged with pilgrims in the wildest state of excitement.

The chapel within the church in which our Lord's tomb is erected has, I think, two, perhaps three or more holes, which are pierced through the walls that support the dome-shaped covering. The pilgrims believe that at a certain moment the Holy Ghost descends in flames of fire, which issue from these holes. Crowds of enthusiastic men, and women, and youths were huddled together in the place surrounding the tomb. Each one had a candle, which he strove to light at the holy flame. The noise they made was deafening. They shouted, "The religion of the Jews is that of dogs; we alone are true!" "The service of the Jews is the service of monkeys, etc., etc.," and this goes on without intermission the whole of the weary hours of waiting. A strong guard of Moslem soldiers which surrounded the tomb had their ranks repeatedly broken by the yelling, seething crowd. They finally linked their arms together, and fought their way back to their places. Our friends said their forbearance and good-humour were wonderful. At length the long-looked-for fire rushed out of the holes, and then the scene during the wild fight to get the candles lighted baffled all description. People in the galleries let down their candles by strings, and got them lit, and soon the whole place was full of lighted candles.

As our friends said, the miracle to them did not consist in the fire, but in the church escaping conflagration. They saw one woman, who had succeeded in lighting her candle, fall back immediately afterwards dead. The excitement was too much for her. Perhaps this moment had been for years the hope of her life. One other death we heard of, that of a boy who was trampled down by the crowd.

We had just returned from a long ride when the triumphant clash of the church bells announced to us that the imposture had been accomplished.

Late that afternoon we wandered up to the Church of the Sepulchre. The precincts and the court in front were crowded with pilgrims, but the church itself was nearly deserted. The floor was slippery with the wax of a thousand tapers. The tomb of our Lord and the various chapels of Greeks, Latins, and Armenians were being illuminated for the great event of the year, the festival of Easter.

With great regret we remembered, on the night of the 25th of April, that it was perhaps the last time we should ever look on that quiet Mount of Olives.

The cries which rose from the street came from pilgrims from every land. The dream of their life had come true, and they were returning **to** their homes, having accomplished the long voyage by sea, and the weary march on land. The music of that Turkish band will fill the air with horrid sounds night after night when these pilgrims are far away, and we have returned to our distant home and country. The question suggests itself: Are these pilgrims satisfied? Are we content? The remembrance of all we have seen cannot pass away. Our pleasant pilgrimage to Jerusalem is over. The recollection of the hours spent in these scenes must leave their mark for ever.

At seven a.m. on the 26th of April we left Jeru**salem.** We had said good-bye the night before to our American friends, and now we parted in the most friendly manner with the attendants at the hotel. The same carriage that had brought us from Jaffa awaited us at the gate. When we engaged it to take us back again, the Italian driver, with many gesticulations, said that he himself was unable to wait on us, but that his wife would drive us, and he added that for two years she had been studying *equitation!* So a stout female was on the box the morning of our departure, and drove us, with great care, to Jaffa.

Before passing the Russian hospice, and at the entrance to the suburbs, we were stopped by a Turkish guard, demanding toll. While Ibrahim was getting out his money, our attention was directed to an old woman on a donkey. The poor old pilgrim refused to pay the toll, declaring she had no money. The Turks became impatient, and hit her donkey over the head, while the muleteer besought her to pay. "Oh! hadgi (pilgrim), pay the men!" But the old lady either would not, or could not do so. I was afraid the "brutal soldiery" would hurt the ancient dame, so I told Ibrahim to pay her toll; and we drove away, leaving all parties satisfied.

The Russian hospice is an immense building, affording accommodation to hundreds of pilgrims. The pilgrims are divided into three classes, the first consisting of the rich Russians, who pay munificently, the second class are those who pay a small fixed sum, and the third are lodged free of any charge. Some of the pilgrims, generally of the second class, have made a **vow** to pass one or two years in the Holy City.

Extending on one side of the road for a long way, there is a line of new houses, solely inhabited by Jews. They live a life totally apart from both the Moslem and the Christian, the followers of both creeds despise them. The Jews' quarter within the walls of Jerusalem is the filthiest part of the city, and the uncleanness of the Jew is a byword. They are unmistakeable in appearance, the men slouching along in what looks like a dressing-gown, their caps are generally surrounded with fur. The long curl the men wear on each side of the face gives them an effeminate appearance. Their features are almost always good, and their complexion fair. Some of the women are very lovely, they are to be seen on a Sunday afternoon sitting by the roadside up near the Russian hospice, watching the people coming and going. One of the saddest sights in Jerusalem is the Jews' wailing-place. Any afternoon they are to be seen. But it is more especially on Friday that they gather under the huge and venerable stones of the old temple wall, and there, with streaming eyes, they call upon the God of Israel to remember His promises to His ancient people.

The stream of pilgrims we passed interested me very much. As we drove down the hill, we overtook long strings of mules and ponies. According to Eastern fashion, the rider and his property were generally on the same animal. It was not, therefore, surprising to pass two of those overladen beasts dead by the wayside. Some of the more wealthy pilgrims had camels to carry their baggage, and we recognised the picture cases whose contents we used to watch being carried about in the holy places at Jerusalem. These pictures are mere daubs, representing the Virgin in golden attire. I believe the Russians venerate them very much.

Once, when we were in the Church of the Holy Sepulchre, we saw a poor Russian carrying in his arms some hideous pictures of the Virgin. He placed them one after another on all the different shrines in the various chapels, and knelt down at each altar. He looked so happy and so hot! His face expressed anxious but delighted faith. This poor man, who had come all the way from far-off Russia to bring these miserable daubs to Jerusalem, was a sight we could not laugh at, for the dream of his life was over, and he would have to toil back again with his treasures to his distant home.

At Latron we again put up at the lonely inn on the hillside, and found the poor waiter suffering from fever and very low-spirited, as Mr. Howard could not dispense with his services till the season was over. After luncheon, we once more got into our little carriage and drove merrily down the hill till we reached Ramleh, where we were pursued by poor lepers, holding up fingerless hands and imploring help, a most awful and dismal sight.

At length we trotted pleasantly into ancient Joppa, and alighted at Howard's Hotel. On entering the hotel, some well-dressed women seemed to be waiting for us. One of them, a very pretty creature, most charmingly dressed, rushed forward, her whole face beaming with delight, seized Ibrahim's hand, and kissed it. He looked so very pleased, and, turning to us, made a graceful salute, saying, "General and my lady, my wife."

We were dismayed to hear that the surf was running very high, and that the hotel people thought we could not get off to the yacht. But we were determined to make an effort to do so, having the full remembrance of the clean and comfortable quarters on board the *Griffin*. Ibrahim was left to bring off the baggage, and my wife and I started for the landing-place, accompanied by a man from the hotel. We were amused to see about forty men in European costume, with fez caps on their heads, sitting *al fresco* at a café near the harbour. They were smoking cigarettes and drinking coffee. It is a curious fact that the smoking of the long Turkish pipe is quite given up now. When I was in the East on a former occasion, at an official visit to any pasha, coffee and long pipes with magnificent mouthpieces were produced; in the present day the pipes are banished, and cigarettes have taken their place. Even the porters and muleteers smoke cigarettes.

When we arrived at the landing-place, a great crowd was assembled lading a ship. We asked for a boat, and the head man told us that there was a very heavy sea on, that he would send us in a boat, but that it was at our own risk, as he considered it unsafe. We were not in duty bound to go, so we returned to the hotel, and from the balcony we could see the *Griffin* pitching and rolling very badly indeed. We dined at the *table-d'hôte*, and met only one other guest, a native doctor, a most intelligent man, in medical charge, as we were informed, of the hospital at Jaffa. The wind howled dismally when we went to bed.

Next morning (27th of April) the sun shone brightly, and the sea was not so rough. Kidby, who had been brought by a yacht's boat from the *Griffin*, made his appearance, and recommended our proceeding at once on board, as the sea generally got up as the day went on. We again went along the cruel pavement, and, as it was very early in the morning, the merchants of Jaffa were not assembled at the café. We, with our camp furniture, got into one of the large native boats with eight oars. We left the little harbour, and went out into the open. The cutter preceded us, but as a big sea was on, and she was occasionally hidden by a huge wave, sometimes we could not see her at all; now and then we got a glimpse of her gracefully cresting a mountain roller. I was rejoiced when we once more trod the *Griffin's* deck, but she was behaving in a most eccentric manner, rolling and tossing like a mad thing. Poor Ibrahim did not look happy.

In reply to my inquiry if he liked the sea, he said, with a sort of apologetic bow,

" No, general; on land, yes; on sea, no!"

The captain welcomed us on board, and ordered steam to be got up. If he had known that we had arrived the night previous, all would have been ready, but no communication had been possible. We had a jolly pitching and tossing for about two hours, a specimen of what those on board had undergone for the last twelve days. The exciting sound of the heaving of the anchor by steam, and the occasional shiver of the screw, gave us notice that we were leaving the roadstead of Jaffa, about the worst anchorage in the Mediterranean.

At one in the afternoon of April the 27th we left Jaffa for Haifa, wind and sea against us. But the day was fine, and we had a beautiful view of the land as we coasted along quite near the shore.

Ibrahim, whose brown cheeks had somehow turned green, occasionally came forward and acted his part as dragoman. He pointed out to us Cæsarea and the Hills of Samaria, but it was hardly fair to ask him questions. It was quite dark when we entered the Bay of Acre. As luck would have it, the wind blew from the north, and right into the place we wanted to anchor off Haifa, which faces St. Jean d'Acre. Had the wind blown from any other point of the compass, we should have had a calm sea, but as it was we pitched and rolled a good deal at anchor. Poor Ibrahim had been asked many questions about the anchorage some time before we had arrived at it, when well out at sea. I suppose feeling unwell had made him bilious, for I heard him answer one question, as to the best place to anchor, in almost furious accents.

"Me do not know the sea, but I think we had better *stope!*"

At length we did "stope," and had a lively night. When we came on deck in the morning it was blowing very fresh, and there was no possibility of landing. The vessels anchored near to us rolled fearfully, so we resigned ourselves to our fate. And there are worse places to be locked up in than a fine yacht, with every comfort on board. In the early morning there was a lull, which was taken advantage of by Ibrahim, who proceeded on shore to make arrangements for our expedition to Nazareth and the Sea of Galilee.

We were lying under Mount Carmel, at the foot of which nestles the town of Haifa. The surf rolled in with the deep, solemn sound the sea often has. In front of us, on the other side of the bay, we could see the walls of Acre. The entrance to the bay was to the left of the town, and the strong, northerly gale swept great waves towards us. To our right was an extent of sandy beach, along which wheeled vehicles passed to and from **Acre**. The river Kishon empties itself into the bay here. We were quite cut off from all communication with the land, owing to the heavy sea. The next day (29th of **April**) was a continuation of the same strong gale and breaking sea. In the evening **a** change of wind took **place**. The sea became calmer, and the night **was fine**.

CHAPTER XI.

IN THE FOOTSTEPS OF CHRIST.

PREPARATIONS FOR OUR START—IBRAHIM INDIGNANT—OUR STEEDS AND THEIR RIDERS—EXPEDITION TO NAZARETH AND THE SEA OF GALILEE—MOUNT CARMEL—APPEARANCE OF THE COUNTRY—THE FIVER KISHON—DESTRUCTION OF TREES IN SYRIA—THE PLAINS OF ESDRAELON—PLOUGHING OPERATIONS—NAZARETH—THE LATIN CONVENT—BROTHER JOHN OF NAZARETH—A VISIT TO VARIOUS MEMORIALS OF CHRIST—MOUNT TABOR—SEA OF GALILEE—TIBERIAS—IBRAHIM'S WOUND.

CHAPTER XI.

AT seven o'clock on the morning of the 30th of April we rowed ashore, and were landed at the steps. A civil merchant received us, and invited us into a long room with leather couches all round it, and windows overlooking the sea, there to wait till everything was ready for **our start**.

We were anxious **to** proceed **on our** journey before the sun got hot. Ibrahim had vanished, but at length I found him in **a** state **of** furious indignation.

"Ah! these peoples, these peoples!" he snarled forth. "I ordered the horses, I paid some moneys —two horses here—one not—ah!"

There were two horses and **a** donkey, besides the baggage animals, but where was the third nag? Time was passing and the sun was getting higher and higher. It was at length decided that my wife was to ride one of the two steeds (it was her horse that was missing), and I was to take the other, while Ibrahim—the Rider of the Desert —was to mount the donkey.

There was nothing to be said against our chargers. Mine was a white old gentleman, who had seen better days, and who retained the bridle of his youth, a magnificent gold-mounted headpiece, with a fearful rusty bit. My wife's mare was a quiet, gentle beast, and Ibrahim's donkey was one of the smallest, with weak hocks, which touched each other. The contrast between the ferocious and indignant Ibrahim, and the mild and docile donkey, was most amusing.

We rode out of the town, which is daily increasing in importance, owing to the number of steamers calling there continually, and exporting great quantities of goods collected by enterprising merchants, who have lately come there.

The road, which goes along the base of Mount Carmel, passes through orchards on first leaving Haifa. We had not gone very far when a man appeared riding the missing horse, a nice young mare, with very showy action. She had wandered up the mountain-side. The saddle was transferred from the donkey, and Ibrahim was once more mounted as he ought to be.

Our road for some miles was quite level, passing through pasture land. Then our path diverged to the left, and, crossing **a** plain where they were making hay, we went **on** to the river Kishon. We saw a long string of camels, which came from Samaria, wending their **way** close under **Mount** Carmel.

Great pools of clear water **lay by** our path, and at one place we crossed **a** rushing stream by **a** low bridge. The water was apparently pure and good, but Ibrahim told **us** it was quite brackish, and my old horse refused to drink it. The plain is marshy, and unsafe to cross in some **parts** farther on, but the ground was firm and secure where we were, and, although there was no decided road, we could trace the marks **of** wheels the whole way.

There is a springless wooden carriage that makes the journey from Haifa to Nazareth, but we missed seeing it, as the last three miles we travelled on horseback are too rocky for it, and **it** has to make a long detour. The country through which we were passing was very different from Judea. There everything was dried up and parched, here the eye rested on lovely green plains and wooded heights, the barley was waving luxuriantly in the soft summer breeze, and up the rugged sides of Carmel brushwood and copse were growing. We reached the ancient river Kishon—a narrow, sluggish stream, with steep clay banks. It is a treacherous river to ford, and we were glad to find a bridge across it. Here it was that Sisera's army was destroyed, after the Battle of Megiddo. "They fought from heaven; the stars in their courses fought against Sisera. The river Kishon swept them away, that ancient river, the river Kishon." (Judges v, 20, 21.)

After we had crossed the bridge, and had ridden on for a short time, the view was most beautiful. Ibrahim pointed out to us on the highest point of Carmel the site which tradition indicates as the place where Elijah built the altar, and fire came down from heaven and licked up the water round the sacrifice, and lower down, on another ridge, where the priests of Baal were slain. Leaving the plain, we began to ascend through a richly-wooded country; the grass was coarse, and, but that it was browner, we might have supposed we were crossing an English park. Great trees raised their branches aloft, and we saw some fine old oaks. It is a sad pity the wanton way the trees in Syria are mutilated and destroyed. Hardly one is allowed to escape. A branch is recklessly lopped off here and there, and a fire is often lit close to the roots, acres and acres of wood being treated in the same fashion.

As we gained the summit of the hill we turned to see the view of Haifa and the blue sea, and then emerging from the trees we saw stretching before us the Plains of Esdraelon. I cannot imagine a finer view. For miles and miles the plain appears a vast field of waving barley, like a calm sea moved by a gentle breeze. There is not a house to be seen, nothing but growing corn. We descended to the plain again and paced along the ground, always keeping the wheel-marks in view, for here various paths diverge. Before us lies Little Hermon, and many places whose names recall Bible stories of great battles and wonderful events.

There was no shade to be had on this part of the road, so at eleven o'clock we turned off across

country to a wooded hill, where we took our
noonday's rest. The horses wandered about,
trying to get nourishment out of the thin, dried
grass and beautiful flowers, with which, towards
the end of April and during the month of May,
the whole country is carpeted. We had heard
much of the beauty of the flowers of Syria, and
nothing we had been told had been overstated.
On this ride there was one specially beautiful
flower that we repeatedly saw, a low-growing,
large, single convolvolus. We were amused and
interested watching the ploughing operations
going on in the fields immediately under the hill
we were bivouacking on. The ploughs are so
light that they are lifted with the greatest ease
into a fresh furrow. The ground seems merely
to require scratching to produce its wonderful
crops. The teams were various. A stately camel
stalked along resignedly with a plough behind it,
a donkey and a cow harnessed together formed
perhaps the most common combination. The
farmer, a son, and a woman generally walked by
a plough, one guiding the animals, another driving the plough, and the third with a measuring
rod keeping the furrows straight. As far as

strangers could judge, they seemed to us a very industrious people. They took no notice of us; they are so accustomed to see travellers from all nations among them.

After getting on our horses again, we still had a couple of miles in the plain, which then merges into valley, soon becoming quite narrow, with high, rocky banks on each side. The number of wild flowers in the glen was surprising. Every now and then the valley became broader, and at these places the people were ploughing the small fields. The whole vale was dotted with diminutive trees, **oak,** and hawthorn, **and** wild rosebushes. Clear rivulets crossed our path, birds were singing happily. We were delighted with the scene. **So** many years of **our** Lord's life having been passed at Nazareth, this haugh so near the town must have been constantly visited by Him. There was a steep climb at the upper end of the valley till we gained the summit, and there before us, lower down on the hill's side, was Nazareth surrounded by hills. The path was difficult for the horses which, with their iron shoes, could find no foothold, especially as in many places there was no road except over the even face of the rock. We walked down the worst part, and then we entered Nazareth by no grand entrance, but through a most filthy farm-yard, where pigs and refuse of all kinds lay on the narrow path.

In single file we passed on our way, but had soon to dismount, the streets were so steep and badly paved. Following Ibrahim, we descended lower and lower till we halted in front of the Latin convent, where we were received most kindly by a monk in his brown cloak, with a rope round his waist. Brother John, whom we found to be a most benevolent and worthy man, led us into the house and upstairs to a very nice apartment, consisting of a well-furnished sitting-room and a clean bed-room opening off it, and welcomed us very warmly to the convent. He left us, but only to return in a few minutes with a large carafe of ice-cold lemonade, which was nectar to thirsty souls after our long ride. We always carried a large waterproof bath with us, and the refreshment of a tub of cold water after a long and dusty ride is wonderful.

When we had dressed, we sat out on the balcony in front of our room. Before us a slope stretched down to a valley looking green and fertile in the spring afternoon. A short distance down this glen rises a hill called the Mount of Precipitation, from which the Jews tried to cast our Lord after His teaching. In the street below us boys were playing at some merry laughing game. Across the street was the gate of the Church **of the** Annunciation, **in the** courts of which we could see the monks moving about. There was a quiet home feeling connected with the green fields and the childish voices of boys at play. A strange feeling of wonder possessed us when we thought that once **our Lord was** a child there, and no doubt entered into all the amusements of His boyhood's time.

Ibrahim came **to** announce dinner. **He** had washed his face and curled his moustache, and, with fez in hand, conducted us **to** the refectory, where our dinner was served.

The house in which we dined was the hospice of the convent, where travellers and pilgrims are received. The monks provide board as well as lodging for those who wish it, making no charge, but accepting what is offered them, on the same principle as the hospices in Jerusalem. An

American said at a *table-d'hôte* that travelling in the Holy Land cost very little, as he had visited no end of convents all over the country and had never been asked to pay one penny.

In our case, having made a bargain with Ibrahim, he fed us, and paid to the convent so much a night for our rooms. There were other pilgrims besides us in the house; but we had our dinner alone, at the upper end of the long table. Brother John received us, and sat down and entertained us with his news. We became great friends, and I shall always remember with a kindly feeling " Brother John of Nazareth."

Later in the evening, as we sat in our rooms, a sound of tom-toms, mixed with men and women's voices, filled the air. I cannot say they were musical voices, but they had a sound of joy. It was a marriage procession. The streets were all illuminated by torches, and the dogs barked, and the children shouted. It was a noisy scene. After a time all was quiet, and as the night went on no sound was heard save the distant bark of a dog.

The 1st of May at Nazareth sounds wondrous sweet and strange! The day was Sunday, and a bright sun was tempered by a fresh, delightful breeze. At breakfast Brother John, in his brown monk's attire, sat beside us and talked to us, telling many traditions of the place. Nazareth, he said, was dreadfully **hot** in summer, being so surrounded by hills that no breeze reaches it. **He** spoke of the Jews as an accursed race, and would not allow that they were ever to return to Jerusalem. He got me to address a letter to **a** lady **in** England, who, with her daughter, had passed some days at Nazareth, and who, from their distant home, had sent him an Easter card, with which he was highly pleased.

After breakfast, we were shown the way to the English Protestant Church, and were surprised to find that the prayers were **in** Arabic. We were afterwards informed that the English congregation had not returned from spending Easter at Jerusalem. Their numbers are very few, consisting principally of the teachers in the schools. When we returned to the convent, we saw from our balcony a marriage procession enter the gates of the church. With **my** glasses, I could see some very lovely faces. **As** they could not see **me,** I had the full benefit of watching their real expression, and they were quite beautiful. They seemed a happy, joyous group as they vanished into the church.

We were summoned by Brother John to go round the sacred places in Nazareth. Through the narrow streets he led us to a chapel, the door of which he unlocked, and, entering, we saw a rock, oblong in shape and very rough. This is called the "Table of Christ," and we were told that the tradition has descended through many generations that our Lord frequently ate at this table with His disciples, both before and after His resurrection. This is written in many languages on the wall. The Empress Helena erected the church over the place, which was destroyed, but has now been rebuilt. We then proceeded to the synagogue where Christ was teaching when they drove Him out, and sought to throw Him from the "brow of the hill." The key was not forthcoming, the rabbi being out, so we continued on our way to the "carpenter's shop" where Joseph gained his bread. All these places are chapels, and the pilgrims who were in Brother John's train devoutly knelt and kissed the various shrines. From the "shop" we went on to the Church of the Annunciation. The part of the convent which was inhabited is divided from the church by the street. A fine gate admitted us into the precincts of the church, which consist of two large, flagged courts. In the one to the back of the church there is erected a large pillar of granite, on the top of which is a gilt statue of the Virgin.

The convent, which is a very large one, is built round the three sides of this court, the church being on the fourth side. It stands on a wide, paved terrace, commanding a fine view of hill and valley, and within is shown the spot sacred to the Annunciation.

Opposite the door, between columns which appear to be under the grand altar, a flight of steps conducts us to a lower altar, with a marble slab beneath it, where the Virgin is said to have stood while the angel spoke with her. Brother John showed us a column which apparently is supported by nothing. Tradition says that the infidels tried to cut it through, but that it is sustained in its place by a miracle. A cave is shown where Mary lived, and a hole in the rock is called her fireplace

The Greek Church have another cave and another rock which they say are the true ones. At Loretto the Church of Rome has the Virgin's Cottage, which was brought there one night by the angels!

Men's traditions are folly. The one reality is that the hills and the valleys are the same as when our Lord ran about in His childhood among the flowers, which no doubt decked then, as they do now, every green spot on the mountains, and where, later in life, He laboured with small success among His townspeople and kinsfolk, for a prophet has little honour in his own country.

In the afternoon we were present during the evening function in the Church of the Franciscans, to which order Brother John belonged. It was the same church in which the Chapel of the Annunciation is situated. The altar was very fine, and the organ was well played. The many worshippers seemed very devout. There was a large party of Italian priests, who had been at Jerusalem, and were now visiting Nazareth. They were residing in our convent, but had their meals at different hours from us. In spite of all the fables told and invented by priests and monks, there is a pleasant reality about Nazareth. The teachings of our childhood are realized here. No place in Palestine seemed more holy and sweet in its associations, totally irrespective of the shrines and chapels.

Early on Monday, the 2nd of May, **our** horses were awaiting us, and, after a six o'clock breakfast, we said farewell to Brother John, who promised to keep our rooms for us, as we intended returning to Nazareth again after visiting Mount Tabor and the Sea of Galilee.

On our way **we** passed the Fountain of the Virgin. There is no doubt that this spring is the same where Mary was wont to go for water. I wish I could say that the young girls we saw there were beautiful. Alas! they were very plain, and several had only one eye! Our ride was through bare hills for some miles. The only person we saw was a little man riding a very wellbred mare, with **a** nice foal following its dam along the stony path. Ibrahim informed me he was "a I doctor," or what we would call an oculist. The people in Syria suffer much from ophthalmia, and **no** doubt his services were much required. The mare and foal were not his property, but were only hired for the day.

After scrambling down a rocky road we came to what once must have been a magnificent forest of oak, but now the appearance the trees present is most distressing, every one, without exception, having been cut all over. There were grand trunks from twelve to fourteen feet high, with a few bunches of green leaves on the top, growing, but dwarfed. This forest of maimed trees continues all the way to the base of Mount Tabor, where a few have escaped the destroyer, and we bivouacked under one. It was a pleasant rest before climbing the hill.

The ascent is very steep, and in some places we had to cross the sheer rock, with a precipice on one side. At length, after a rather tiresome scramble, we reached the summit. There are very extensive ruins everywhere, ruins of castles and churches. The Latin convent crowns the summit of the mountain, and the Greek convent stands on a lower level. Though built within a stone's throw of each other, the convents have no dealings together. Both have done all they can to ruin the appearance of the place. Stiff walls have been erected everywhere, to preserve the one from the encroachments of the other—truly a sad sight to see.*

We were received courteously by the Latin monk, who was of a more retiring disposition than Brother John of Nazareth. He showed us our rooms, clean and plainly furnished, and then disappeared. Ibrahim came and took us to the ruins of an ancient church recently opened up. We scrambled up into a turret, and were charmed with the view. As Mount Tabor stands alone and has a round top, the view from any side is most extensive. At its foot are the Plains of Esdraelon. From where we were seated, as it were in the gallery of a theatre, we could see the ridge of Carmel, Little Hermon, Nain, and

* "For centuries Mount Tabor has been considered the scene of the transfiguration of our Lord, and convents have been built asserting this to be the case; but the top of Mount Tabor has from time immemorial been a fortified and inhabited spot. Thirty years after this time, Josephus on this very mountain strengthened the existing fortress of Itaburion. This, therefore, was not the spot to which Jesus could have taken the three apostles 'apart by themselves.' Mount Hermon seems to have been the sacred place, the 'Mount Hermon' of Jewish poetry. Its very name means 'the mountain,' and the scene which it witnessed would well suffice to procure for it the distinction of being the only mountain to which in Scripture is attached the epithet 'holy.'"—Farrar's "Life of Christ."

Endor. The lingering sun cast long shadows over the green expanse before us. It was a peaceful scene now; but what battles had been fought on that plain! and fancy pictured the army assembled here which was to defeat Sisera and drive his warriors into the river Kishon. "Go and draw towards Mount Tabor, and take with thee ten thousand men of the children of Naphthali and the children of Zebulon, and I will draw unto thee to the river Kishon Sisera, the captain of Jabin's army, with his chariots and his multitude, and I will deliver him into thine hand." *

And there, nestling under that hill, is Nain, where our Lord brought to life again the dead man, "the only son of his mother, and she was a widow," and still farther is Endor, where Saul went to see the witch when he came from the fountain of Jezreel.

After remaining some time, fascinated with this most interesting panorama, we scrambled down from our high perch among the ruins and took a short walk among the remains of the crusades, churches, and fortifications, and then

---

* Deborah to Barak, Judg. iv, 3, 7.

we returned to dinner in a very long room, more like a mess-room than the refectory of a convent. We were soon glad to retire to our own rooms, where everything was so perfectly clean that we enjoyed an *untortured* sleep.

We were up before daylight to see the sun rise. The air was quite cold, and a breeze was blowing gently when we first emerged from our rooms. The eastern sky was just assuming a pink glow, and the mountains of Gilead were still dark and gloomy; but in a short time a rosy light brightened the distant view. Hermon appeared tipped with snow, towering above all. At first the mountain seemed to wake up from its sleep, so grey and clouded it was, but all of a sudden the rays of the coming sun played around its majestic head, and with, as it were, a shout of joy, it glowed in brightness, first rosy and sweet, then dazzling with light.

Then a blue line came out on the view—the Sea of Galilee, and as the morning became clearer the whole distance, from where we stood to that blue line, seemed like a green park dotted with trees. Finally a curtain of clouds dropped over the scene, and we could see no more.

The time for our departure being come, we shook hands with the monk and bade him farewell. The path was so steep that we walked down the mountain, the monks having made a path the whole way. At the foot we turned to the right and continued our journey through grand old oaks, dwarfed by the relentless hands of Turks and Bedouins. After two hours' ride we came to two very ancient buildings, loop-holed for defence; they are called the Merchants' Khan, Khan-el-Tujjar. Ibrahim told us they were erected for the protection of travellers on their way to Egypt, as at one time the tribes were "very great robbers." We had hardly passed these old ruins when we overtook a long line of camels moving slowly, accompanied by the usual donkey, without which they never seem to travel. It was a pleasant ride among the cornfields and green pastures. We came to a turn in the way, for we had arrived at the caravan road from Damascus to Jerusalem and Egypt. Near here are deep wells which Ibrahim said were never dry. Some picturesque figures were gathered round them watering their flocks. A little farther on we saw on our left a curious shaped hill called the Kuràn Hattin, the Horns of Hattin, towards which the ground rises. There is little doubt that this is the hill where our Lord went to pray, and continued all night in prayer to God, and where He addressed the multitude.*

On this same Kuràn Hattin was fought, on the 5th of July, 1187, a decisive battle between the Crusaders and Saladin, in which the Christians were totally defeated, and all Palestine was conquered by the Moslems.

We rode on, and soon came in full view of the Sea of Galilee, many hundred feet below us, and the old ruined tower of Tiberias clinging to the shore. The Lake of Tiberias is most interesting,

---

* "The scene of this lonely vigil and of the Sermon on the Mount was in all probability the singular elevation known at this day as the Kurân Hattin, or Horns of Hattin. It is a hill with a summit which closely resembles an oriental saddle, with two high peaks. On the west it rises very little above the level of a broad and undulating plain ; on the east it sinks precipitately towards a plateau on which lies, immediately beneath the cliffs, the village of Hattin, and from this plateau the traveller descends through a wild and tropical gorge to the shining levels of the Lake of Galilee. It is the only conspicuous hill on the western side of the lake, and is singularly adapted by its conformation both to form a place for short retirement and a rendezvous for gathering multitudes."—Farrar's "Life of Christ."

and, like Nazareth, connected with the happiest time of our Lord's life. On the shores of that lake He collected His apostles, and on that quiet-looking sea He often sailed. We descended by a very steep path to Tiberias, the walls of which are picturesque in their ruin. Earthquakes and time have shaken them so much that in some places the gaps are so great that cattle were going in and out through them.

We now began to feel the excessively close heat which makes Tiberias so unhealthy, and, when we arrived at the convent, my wife had an attack of fever which prevented her from moving out of her room. The Superior of the convent was very attentive and courteous. He took us up a stair into a long corridor, on each side of which were many doors opening on to it, and above every door a verse of Scripture was painted. Our room was here, and looked out into the street. The beds had no mosquito curtains, and the one small window let in more sun than air. At the end of the long corridor was a large window, opening upon a little garden, immediately beyond which was the Sea of Galilee. The view of the abrupt and sterile country on the opposite coast was very extensive. When our Lord was upon the earth, Tiberias was a great city, and the Sea of Galilee was covered with fleets of boats, and its shores by towns and villages. Now it is a small place, peopled by a miserable collection of Jews, who are the dirtiest of the dirty, and a few boats are the only representatives of its former greatness.

My wife could not come with us, but Ibrahim and I got a boat and went for a sail. When we left, the sea was very calm, and a nice breeze filled our sails. We coasted towards the Jordan, and passed the camping-ground, where four camps were pitched, with distinguishing flags—French, Austrian, Belgian, and English. A short distance farther on, and we came to the warm baths. There are two buildings, but both in a ruinous state. These warm springs are mentioned by Pliny and Josephus. Numbers of people were lounging about. Some were arriving and others leaving, mounted on horses and camels. Ibrahim informed me that the season for bathing had just begun, and that it lasted for about two months, during which time crowds of people come from the surrounding country to bathe. As I was alone, I did not care to go any farther. I had had a sail on the Sea of Galilee! We put about, and returned to Tiberias. The lake, which had been so calm, now broke in little waves, the wind came in gusts, and before we landed the sea had got up, and we were buffeted about in fine style. I was glad that it was so, for it confirmed the Bible account of the sudden approach of these storms.

I found my wife not at all well; the heat was oppressive, and the mosquitoes were very trying. I passed an anxious night. Morning broke fine, and my great hope was that, if we could get up the hill into the cool air, we should get above the fever regions. Dressing and starting required a great effort; but once on horseback, and every minute getting higher up the mountain, and feeling the cool morning breeze, helped my wife to sit her horse for four hours. She fought gallantly against the fever, and finally won the battle, though it left her very exhausted.

The ascent from the lake is very steep, but at length we reached the top. Our road was the same as on the day before till we came to the ancient wells, when, instead of turning to the left, which would have taken us to Mount Tabor, we continued straight on. The sun was high in the heavens, and very powerful before we came to our halting-place, under the shade of some olive-trees, near Cana of Galilee. My wife was glad to have a rest, though it was not very luxurious lying in a ploughed field, with the sun flickering through the olive foliage above us. In the afternoon we rode through Cana. Of course there are disputes as **to** whether this village was the real place where our Lord's first miracle happened. It is now a ruined hamlet. There is a fountain below it, where the water-jars were filled. **It** is prettily situated in a valley, with green trees about it. We passed on, and had a great climb up a steep hill over Nazareth, **whence the** view was very extensive. We descended the stony road past the Virgin's Fountain, and once more were welcomed by Brother John into **the** comfortable Latin Convent at Nazareth.

Early next morning we said a kindly farewell to the friendly monk, who seemed quite sorry **to** part with us, and it was with a feeling of sadness that we bade a final adieu to Nazareth. When we reached the top of the hill **a** strong breeze was blowing from the north, so we rather expected a rough sea in the Bay of Haifa. The descent of the mountain was done more quickly than the ascent. Our horses had improved in condition, so that this, our last ride, was very pleasant. Our road lay through the same fields we had crossed before, and we saw the same people ploughing in them. The plains of Esdraelon were rich with ripening crops. We halted for luncheon under a very fine olive-tree in the forest above the plain, and then we mounted our horses and proceeded onwards.

Passing through the valley, before arriving at the bridge over the river Kishon, we met two most ruffianly-looking men, armed with guns, and carrying great bludgeons. They eyed us as we passed, but they saw we had weapons too. Meeting these men, I asked Ibrahim if travellers like ourselves ought not always to carry arms?

"My general," he replied, "all the years I have wandered I never was attacked. But there are bad *mens*. I might be. It is sometime done!"

Ibrahim had a great wound on his forehead, and he told me how he had received it. His parents were Christians, and his native village was in the mountains near Damascus. In 1860 he was a boy, and a very bad feeling sprang up between the Christians and Mohammedans. Some fights had taken place on several occasions. The Christians were getting the worst of it, so the people of his village went to Osman Pasha, and applied for help. The Pasha told them that they would be safe in a large barracks, if they gave up their arms. This they did. Then the Druses came and murdered all they could. Ibrahim's father, mother, and brother were killed. He was shot at, and the bullet scarred his forehead very deeply, and he showed me his wrist, which bore the marks of a bayonet wound. He escaped death in a marvellous manner. Lord Dufferin was sent out by the British Government, and, owing to his representations, Osman Pasha was hanged. A very insecure feeling exists among the Christian population. The Moslems are quiet now, but a spark would rouse them again. Such was the purport of Ibrahim's story.

We arrived at Haifa in the afternoon; a strong breeze and heavy sea were making the *Griffin* dance at her anchor. The civil merchant got us a large shore-boat with about ten boatmen. On our way to the yacht, one of these heroes caught a crab, and went heels over head! The big sea that was running made this escapade not altogether a good joke, but in process of time we once more trod the deck of the *Griffin*, and were welcomed back by Captain Oman and all the crew. We had a very rough night, but the pleasure of being back once more counterbalanced the inconvenience of a rolling ship.

CHAPTER XII.

THE LEBANON AND ANTI-LEBANON.

ST. JEAN D'ACRE—CROSS-GRAINED TURKS—THE TYRIAN LADDER—TYRE—PROPHECIES CONFIRMED—SIDON—BEYROUT—LADY HESTER STANHOPE—ECCENTRIC COACHMAN—WE PART WITH IBRAHIM—IBRAHIM DEHRONY—TRADITION OF ST. GEORGE—THE ORIENTAL HOTEL—START FOR DAMASCUS—ASCENT OF LEBANON—CHALCIS—VALLEY OF WADY-EL-KURN—THE RIVER ADANA—THE ANTI-LEBANON—APPROACH TO DAMASCUS.

CHAPTER XII.

AT seven a.m. on the 6th **of** May we left Haifa, and steamed over to St. Jean d'Acre. The passage across took only about an hour. **We anchored** outside the harbour. A ruined tower still remains, shattered by the round shot of the fleet under Admiral Stopford and Commodore Napier in 1840. **A** long line of fortifications looks towards the sea; but the town **has** a ruined appearance. We landed after luncheon, and were met by the consul's cavass, with offers of assistance. I was anxious to go up to the fortifications, but on applying for permission to the commanding officer it was refused, so we walked through the bazaar, and went to the old mosque. The cavass took us to see the graves of **two** British officers, Major Oldfield, Royal Marines, who was killed in a sortie, in 1799, against Napoleon, and

Colonel Walker, Royal Marines, aged 68, who died in 1840. The tombs are of marble; but the natives are no respecters of the dead, for stone and *débris* were accumulated round those old warriors' resting-places. There are few sadder sights than these lonely graves, found all over the world, where the soldiers and sailors of Britain have served their sovereign and country.

As we were not admitted into the fortifications there was not much to see, so we returned on board the yacht. They are a cross-grained lot at Acre. The commandant insisted on our papers being produced, though we had now been lying at Haifa, close by, for a long time; but that did not signify. So the captain, who was on shore, had to hurry off to the *Griffin* and bring the documents required.

A beautiful moonlight night succeeded a warm day. At three a.m. on the 7th of May we steamed away from St. Jean d'Acre. I got up at dawn to see the sun rise from behind the mountains of Phœnicia. As we passed near the shore we could see the path up what is called the "Tyrian Ladder." The morning crept on, and so did our lively craft, making slow way against a contrary wind. Villages and **towns** appeared before us along the coast, and gradually faded away in the distance. As we left them, our interest increased when we got near Tyre. The captain shared in our feeling about this place, which, in the old time, was the great seaport of the world. **We** kept close in shore, and had **a** very good view of all that remains of this once prosperous city. Most picturesque, **no** doubt, it is; but it is strange to think that this was once the mistress of the seas. How literally **the** prophecies against Tyre have been fulfilled. All her grand fleet **now** consists of **a few** fishing-boats **we** could see **drawn up on** the shore. Now no vessel the size **of the** *Griffin* could **get close** under the town, **for** the sand has choked the harbour. "**And** they shall make a spoil **of** thy riches and make a prey of thy merchandise, and they shall break down thy walls and destroy thy pleasant houses, and they shall lay thy stones and they timber and thy dust in the midst of the water, and I will make thee like the top of a rock, thou shalt be a place to spread nets upon, thou shalt be built no more."*

* Ezek. xxvi. 12. 14.

There could not be a better description of this fallen queen than these prophecies spoken of her in the time of her grandeur. On the old ruined walls we saw nets spread to dry in the sun.

As we passed on, Ibrahim pointed out a village on the mountain side: this was Sarepta, where Elijah went from the brook Cherith, and saw the woman gathering sticks, who made him a cake.* From the deck of the yacht we could not see much, but the mountains were there, and the view was the same as in the days of Elijah.

And now we drew near to Sidon, which did not seem in quite such a ruinous condition. Sidon is a very ancient city, and is mentioned in Genesis x, 19. Joshua calls it Zidon the Great, xix, 23. It was celebrated for its arts, and now is a small and half ruinous village. We could see the citadel, a time-worn tower, and lower down, near the harbour, on the rocks, an ancient castle. But ruined walls were everywhere. The environs seemed fertile, and we saw gardens and fruit-trees. Once Sidon was a great harbour for merchandise, but now all trade is gone to Beyrout.

A few miles farther on, high up in the moun-

* 1 Kings, xvii, 3, 24.

tains, Ibrahim drew our attention to a large white building. This was the convent where Lady Hester Stanhope passed the last days of her life, and where she died, and is buried in the garden.

For a long time we had seen before us a point of land round which we must steer before arriving at the end of our day's voyage. It is curious how long it takes to arrive at a certain point seen for hours from the deck of a ship. But at length we made the long-looked-at cape, and were delighted with the picturesque appearance of Beyrout. Far off in the mountains which encircle the bay, trees are to be seen with a glass, the celebrated cedars of Lebanon.

The town of Beyrout is finely situated, but if we hoped to have a quiet anchorage we were mistaken. A Turkish man-of-war lay near us, and a French frigate was also anchored not far off. The wind blew into the harbour, and a heavy swell was rolling in, which lasted all the time the *Griffin* was at Beyrout.

The day after we arrived was Sunday, the 8th of May, and, pratique having been procured the day before, we landed in the morning for church.

Kidby had ordered a carriage to meet us at the landing, so we drove up the hill to the Protestant Church. It appears that the Presbyterian and Episcopalian forms of worship are held on alternate Sundays. This Sunday was devoted to the Presbyterians.

After the service was over, as the post-office did not open till one o'clock, we took a short drive, and then returned on board with our letters.

And here we were to part with Ibrahim, as our future journey to Damascus was to be made by carriage. My wife and I were quite sorry to part with this intelligent little man. We paid his passage back to Jaffa. He was to leave by the Russian steamer, which went off that afternoon. Ibrahim Dehrony is always to be heard of at Howard's Hotel, Jaffa.

Next day, May 9th, we landed in the afternoon, and took up our quarters at the Oriental Hotel. Our rooms looked out on the sea, we were immediately above it, and there was the *Griffin* tossing about in the troubled Mediterranean.

We had engaged the *coupé* of the diligence, which leaves Beyrout for Damascus at four a.m.

every morning. After luncheon we took a carriage and drove to the old mosque, on the site where tradition places St. George's fight with the dragon. Hundreds of years ago it was a Christian church, now it is a Moslem mosque. There is an old well close by over which is built an ancient cupola. It appears that after the fight the saint's sword was naturally very bloody, so he thrust it into the soft ground to cleanse it, and lo! a spring of water came forth—hence the well. The scenery round Beyrout is very luxuriant, and the many houses surrounded by trees are pleasing to look upon. Many mulberries grow everywhere, and silk is a great staple.

It is only very lately that carriages have been started at Beyrout, so the drivers are most eccentric. Our coachman was dressed in the usual white linen Turkish blouse, with a fez on his head. He gathered up his reins in a bundle, and shouted at his little horses. Away they went at full gallop, up hill and down dale; round corners, through narrow lanes, our mad Jehu flourished his whip, and screamed fiercely. Fortunately we were not upset, nor did we run over anybody, which was marvellous.

The Oriental Hotel is very comfortable, and the cuisine is not bad, but there is one very great nuisance. Innumerable beggars, in every state of squalor and disease, throng the entrance, and force themselves on the notice of the stranger in a most revolting manner, and no one can enter or leave the hotel without being attacked by these poor, wretched creatures.

At half-past two o'clock in the morning of the 10th of May a knock at our door announced the unpleasant fact that we must get up and dress. It was a lovely night, with a cool, fresh breeze from the sea. In the East there seems to be no regular time for sleep. Servants call one and bring breakfast at three o'clock in the morning, just as much as a matter of course as the servants call you at eight o'clock at home. And it certainly is much easier to get up at unearthly hours there than in the West. One has not the same "shivery" feeling that an early start at home produces. We were able to do justice to an excellent breakfast before we started. We stepped out into the dark, glad to find that the beggars were not there, and got into the carriage with the reckless driver. We had not more than a mile to drive, chiefly through the bazaar, to the place from whence the diligence starts.

According to the French manner of doing things, *messieurs les voyageurs* are ordered to be at the office half an hour before *le départ*, so we found all our fellow-passengers assembled. A very civil man in authority begged us to be seated in the stuffy little waiting-room; he was desirous of knowing if I was a relation of a Maxwell, an engineer, whose dragoman he had been while the English were carrying on the work of bringing water from the Dog River to Beyrout—it is now in the hands of the same company, and Beyrout is one of the few towns on the coast where the water is really good and safe to drink. We preferred strolling up and down under the stars, watching the faint light of day rapidly increasing, till it was time to start.

At last the team of three horses and three mules were ready, and we climbed up into the *coupé*, much congratulating ourselves on having engaged the whole of it. The coachman cracked his whip and said, "Eiogh!" in true French fashion, and we were off. We trotted at a very good pace for several miles along the first-rate road made by a French company, which continues the whole way to Damascus equally good. We were surprised to see how very little traffic there was on it; long lines of laden waggons we passed belonging to the company, and an occasional gaily-dressed horseman, but the stream of donkeys and camels generally to be met with followed the rocky pathway, often at no great distance from the highway. Much puzzled by the perverse nature of a people preferring a difficult track to a well-made road, we put it down to the stolidity of the Turk, who sees no good in anything new. But in this case we wronged him. A heavy toll on each loaded beast is the cause of the preference for old paths to new roads.

The sun was rising when we began the ascent of Lebanon. It took five hours' continued strain on the collar. The view was perfectly beautiful. On the mountain sides were gardens and vineyards innumerable, and as the sun rose the soft tints on green trees and brown rocks were marvellous. Far off, as we turned a sharp corner, we could see behind us, like tiny spots, the ships at anchor in the bay; before us the highest peaks of Lebanon were white with snow. When we arrived at the summit, we immediately began the descent on the other side by the most wonderfully engineered road, all zig-zags, till we came to a broad plain, through which we trotted at the merriest of paces. We halted half-way at a nice country inn among trees, where we had quite a French *déjeûner*, and, after an hour, the time to start was signalled by the old familiar cry, "**En** voiture, mesdames et messieurs!"

We had a long trot over a regular French road, straight as an arrow, till we got to Chalcis, a ruined city, and then past Mejdel, where a temple is seen. After a time we came to Wady-el-kurn, a valley three miles long, with the wildest scenery imaginable. Once the abode of robbers, it is now the resort of shepherds with their flocks of goats. When we drove through one of the **narrowest** parts, a picturesque figure jumped into the centre of the road with a look of "stand and deliver!" on his face. He was armed with a long gun, but I presume he was peaceably inclined, for a great talk ensued, which ended in **a** goat **being** caught and milked, and a bowl of milk being handed up to our coachman.

After emerging from the valley, we ascended a steep hill, and then drove along a very sterile plain. The sun was powerful, and the heat made us sleepy. The oft-repeated question, "I wonder how far we have to go now?" was followed by a yawn, when all of a sudden, at a turn of the road, we left desolation behind us, and found ourselves in fairyland.

We were on the banks of a swift-running river among green trees, and there was the perfume of flowers instead of the smell of dust. The remainder of our journey was delightful. We entered a narrow gorge; on one side we had high rocks above us, in every crevice of which grew ferns, and flowering shrubs, and graceful trees. The sound of rushing water was everywhere. The Abana flowed clear as crystal on the other side of the road, and kept us company all the way to Damascus. Beyond the river were luxuriant woods, and above all towered the mountains of Anti-Lebanon. We forgot the fatigue of our long drive and the dreary plain as we experienced the full beauty of the scene. As we got nearer to Damascus we met gaily-dressed Moslems mounted on showy horses. At first they were dignified enough, but as our great dilly approached them, we were too much for the high-spirited Arabs. They turned and fled, and the graceful riders became ordinary mortals.

In the green fields that border the river Abana near the city well-bred mares and foals were grazing, and on the river's bank were seated groups of Mahometans who gazed at our dust-covered vehicle with great disdain. Damascus, with its gleaming white domes and minarets, now appeared close before us. We passed numbers of cafés by the water-side, in which Turkish officers were smoking cigarettes, and watching the horses swimming in the river. Apparently all the horses of Damascus are groomed in the waters of the Abana. Naked grooms urged their chargers into the deepest places, and with shouts and gesticulations forced them to swim. The horses probably have been trained to this all their lives, as they did not seem to offer much resistance.

And now we turned sharply to the right, and, crossing the river by a low bridge, we trotted through a gateway into a large open court crowded with people, who gave a shout of welcome as our guard sounded a triumphant note on his rather cracked brass trumpet. And thus we arrived at Damascus.

CHAPTER XIII.

DAMASCUS

DAMASCUS COMPARED WITH CONSTANTINOPLE—OUR HOTEL—THE FAIR—BAZAARS OF THE DIFFERENT TRADES—THE BRASS BAZAAR—THE GRAND MOSQUE—STREET CALLED STRAIGHT—PROSTRATE COLUMNS—HOUSE OF ANANIAS—THE GATE EAST OF DAMASCUS—SCENE OF PAUL'S CONVERSION—PERSECUTION OF CHRISTIANS—GRAVE OF FATIMA THE DAMASCAN—HOUSES OF THE WEALTHY INHABITANTS—THE PUBLIC GARDENS—CIRCASSIAN REFUGEES—DRIVE AMONG THE BANKS OF THE ABANA—ARRIVAL AT BEYROUT

CHAPTER XIII.

WHEN we stepped down from the diligence, we bade adieu to western scenes, all became eastern. Constantinople is not so thoroughly oriental in appearance as Damascus, and in one respect the latter city is far superior to the former. Damascus is very clean, and there are no bad smells or mangy dogs as in Constantinople. Pariahs there are, but each one seems to belong to the shop in front of which it basks.

We were conducted to the hotel by an English-speaking dragoman, who at once claimed us as his property, presenting a note from the Commodore's party, who had only left Damascus the day before, recommending him as a capital guide. The distance is not more than five minutes' walk from where the diligence stops. We entered the hotel by a wicket-gate, bending low, and found ourselves in a court shaded by trees, in the centre of which was a large fountain surrounded with flowers, with a jet d'eau, the sound of whose falling water was very pleasant on that hot day. A very stately landlady, who spoke no language but Arabic, gave orders to the dragoman, but took no notice of us. We were shown into a delightfully clean bed-room looking on the court in which the fountain always played. We at first demurred about sleeping on the ground-floor, but were told that the best rooms upstairs had been secured by telegraph for an American party. We might, however, go up and judge for ourselves whether the bed-rooms that remained were as good as the one that had been assigned to us, and the result of our exploration was that we thankfully came back to the room below. It was a contrast to the squalid rooms perched on the top of rickety wooden stairs in various parts of the upper building. We were conveniently situated for the *table-d'hôte*, as it was on the side of the court opposite us, and on the ground-floor was also the drawing-room, with its beautiful fountain of clearest water in the centre, and the silver drinking-cup beside it.

This was a charming novelty. When we entered the door, before you was this beautiful spring in its marble bowl. On each side were elevated floors of marble, very prettily furnished with rich carpets, divans, and tables. The walls and ceilings were handsomely decorated; there was a freshness about this place I never saw rivalled, and, as mosquitoes are unknown at the time of the year when we were there, we enjoyed thoroughly the perfumed coolness of the air.

On the morning after our arrival we started with our dragoman to see the sights of the place. We passed through the square of the town, where the horse-bazaar is situated. A mob of wild horses had been driven in from far away pastures. Many of them were mares, with foals at their feet, huddled together in graceful groups, looking with alarmed defiance at their surroundings. Besides the wild, untrained animals there were plenty of nice-looking nags for sale.

From this horse-fair we passed into the brass-bazaar. Damascus is famed for its brass work. We bought some beautiful trays in embossed work, a very curious old lamp, and some bowls. Our dragoman made the bargain for us. The scale on which he paid seemed to be rather below the half of what was asked. My wife took a fancy to a fakeer's wallet in brass, but declined to give fifteen francs for it. As the merchant seemed to think her offer of five francs beneath contempt we walked on, but swift repentance fell upon him, and he pursued us with the article. After that, I lost confidence in my former plan of always paying half of what was asked.

Every trade has its own bazaar, and you may walk miles in them. The inlaid-work of mother-of-pearl on wood is another *specialité* of Damascus. We bought several specimens of the work. They make most lovely little tables, glistening with mother-of-pearl. The price asked for these is very great. And there are chests, cradles, and wardrobes all in the same style, but these larger articles are quite beyond the capacities of a traveller's luggage. From this bazaar we passed into "the street that was called straight," which runs east to west, and is about one mile long. The bazaars are broad, and very clean, and no disagreeable smells annoyed us. There is plenty of room for the strings of donkeys and occasional camels to pass without jostling. The people are perfectly civil, and show no curiosity, in fact, we stare a good deal more at them than they do at us. The women are almost all veiled. In their own quarter, the Christian part of the population do not veil, but they yield to the prejudice of the Moslems when they go among them.

The saddlers have a very bright street of their own, with gaily ornamented trappings and gorgeous horse-gear of all kinds. We saw gem-studded saddle-cloths and costly headstalls. Then we came to the shoemaker's bazaar. Even it was bright with red and yellow slippers and brilliant sandals. The English bazaar was not interesting to us, though it seemed to be doing a very brisk trade. Gaudy felt carpets were in great request that special morning. We could only wonder at the taste of people who had the soft, rich, perfectly-blended tints of Persia so constantly before their eyes. The bazaars are very interesting, but there is a degree of sameness about them. Constantinople, Cairo, Damascus are very much the same, only the latter is free from all the horrors which even Cairo is not altogether without.

After some hours' exploration we gladly agreed

to our dragoman's suggestion that, if we were to be in time for the twelve o'clock breakfast at the hotel, we had better turn homewards.

A few carriages are to be had for hire at Damascus. There is really only one road fit for wheels, the highway to Beyrout, but, as Demetri assured us, "if we went slow" we might go to many places. We told him to go to his dinner, desiring him to be at the door with a carriage at three o'clock. It was not a bad little trap which he brought, with a roof and curtains, for the sun was very hot, even so far north as Damascus, and so early in the year. Nothing could be more unlike a carriage road than that which led to the places to which we went. Our dragoman took his own way, and showed us many places interesting only from association with past history. The Great Mosque cannot be entered without an order, but we were permitted to look in at the door. It is built on the site of the house of Rimmon, where Naaman attended his master.[*] A heathen temple therefore stood here, which afterwards became a Christian church, and is now a Moslem mosque.

[*] 2 Kings, v, 18.

The "street called straight," no doubt, is the same as in the days of Paul, but the houses are all more modern. The houses in old times had columns in front of them, many of which, now fallen, lie prostrate on the ground. Near the west end of the street we were invited to descend to see the house of Ananias, the disciple who saw a vision,* and came to Paul.† We left our carriage and followed our guide past the bare, sun-dried, mud-walled houses of the Christian quarter, to a door by which we entered into a court, and from thence went down to the house of Ananias, which has the appearance of a vault, but is fitted up with a altar, and is used as a place of worship. The inevitable backsheesh was given to a woman who appeared at the right moment, and we went back to the "street called straight," to the carriage.

At the west entrance of this street is a very ancient gate, "Bab-el-Jabyeh," which has been partly built up for nearly a thousand years. Out by this gate we passed beyond the walls of the city to the green belt of orchards that surround it. The jolting got beyond endurance, and we

* Acts ix, 10.   † Acts xxii, 12.

found that, except for the name of having a carriage, we might as well have walked. We were bound for the spot where St. Paul heard the voice that stopped him on his career of persecution. The old Roman road that existed in those days is all destroyed except a few yards, which mark the exact place of the scene of Paul's conversion. Close to this is the native Christian cemetery where the victims of the massacre in 1860 were buried. It is a dreary, uncared-for, sun-baked region, where every other place is so green and bright.

"Ah! sir, these were fearful times," said our dragoman, as he looked sadly on the crumbling graves. "The Christians who were murdered were buried there in one large grave—all, *except those who were eaten by the dogs.*"

This dragoman, like Ibrahim, was a Christian, and had been wounded. He told most wonderful stories of his escape, and they might be true; but he must have been very young in 1860. One was about his grandfather, an old man of eighty-three. The Moslems came to him, and called on him to abjure Christianity. The old man asked for a few moments to consider, and devoted the time to prayer. Then this old hero called to his persecutors, and said: "Now I am ready to die, in the name of the Father, and of the Son, and of the Holy Ghost!" and then they hacked him to pieces.

Passing on from there we soon stood again under the walls of the city. The tower is shown from which St. Paul was let down in a basket. Tradition says that the porter who helped him to escape was put to death, and that he lies in the Christian burying-ground, in which his grave is much reverenced. The English cemetery is not far from here. There are two graves of remarkable men there, Dr. William Arnold Bromfield, and the historian, H. T. Buckle.

Entering the city again by the gate, our dragoman proposed taking us to see some of the houses belonging to the wealthy inhabitants, who are most good-natured in allowing strangers to go over their dwellings. It must be worse than living in a show-place at home, for there private rooms are safe from intrusion, but at Damascus every door is thrown open.

Our first visit was paid to a Greek merchant's house. We drove through a narrow street till we came to a very mean door, at which our dragoman knocked, and we were admitted. We passed first into a small yard, and then another door was opened, and we were ushered into a magnificent court surrounded by rooms opening into it. The pavement was all marble, inlaid with mosaic. On one side there was a raised marble platform of the purest white, with a flight of steps in the centre. We ascended these, and entered a very tastefully-furnished reception-room, in which the sight and sound of falling water gave a delicious sense of freshness. A large marble tank of perpetually running water, clear as crystal, was at one end of the room. A richly-chased, silver drinking-cup tempted one to drink, and surely there can be no purer, sweeter water than that of the Abana.

There were two more drawing-rooms; the one on the left was most gorgeous, all the fittings and hangings being oriental, with the exception of the carpet, and there they failed, for the floor, instead of being covered with their own beautiful Persian rugs, was covered with a French carpet, very handsome of its kind, but not in harmony with the other things. The drawing-room on the right was called the European room. The furniture was all French, and the wardrobe with the glass door was very fine, if not quite in its proper place. The lady of the house, the Greek merchant's wife, received us dressed as for a ball, with splendid diamonds in her hair. She apologized for not being able to go round the house with us, as the Greek Patriarch was dining with **her,** so she gracefully bowed herself away, leaving her son, a **boy** of ten or twelve, to do the honours.

The boy was delighted, and waved us to come with him. We expected to be shown valuable pieces of sculpture, or some rare pictures; but, the boy's thoughts being otherwise occupied, he conducted us into a dark passage, and then to a window looking into a room, and, **with** a face radiant with delight, said, "Look!" and there, to our confusion, was seated the lady of the diamonds, with about thirty guests, among whom **was** the Greek Patriarch. They seemed very jolly, and champagne was being handed round in profusion. Of course we beat a retreat in haste, but we had time **to** observe **the** beauty of the room, which was large enough to be a very grand ball-room. **Our** youthful guide was, I fancy, disgusted at our not being more excited by the sight of so many good things to eat and drink.

From hence we passed into a perfect little flower-garden at the back, completely ablaze with flowers, and the air sweet with orange-blossoms and rare shrubs. Our young host made a little posy for each of us, and presented it with a graceful bow and that easy grace which is so natural to all classes in the East. We soon after went back to our carriage. Backsheesh must be given to some one, but the fashion in this house was to drop it into a box at the door "for the servants."

We paid a visit to another Greek merchant's house, quite as grand as the former. We saw the ladies of the house and some visitors, rather nice-looking girls, lounging on sofas smoking narguilehs. They were very civil, and showed us round the place. It was on the same principle as the last abode we saw—a vast marble court, with magnificent rooms surrounding it. In one of the drawing-rooms, on a richly-carved table, there was a silver flagon, with drinking-cups like "quaighs." One of the ladies insisted I should

have some of the contents of the bottle, which I
accepted, and drank their healths. The liqueur
was " Mastique."

After having seen over this house, we were taken
to the public gardens, a perfect place in which
to spend hours on a hot summer's day. The trees
throw masses of shade on walks and alleys. Little
rivulets trickle in all directions, and one of the
many branches of the Abana tears along at the
end of the garden. The Christian part of the
population come here a great deal on Sundays
and fête days, and this is the place to see them.

Next day we had another morning in the
bazaars, spending a long hour bargaining for
Persian carpets. We carried off three, paying for
them with Napoleons, and it is characteristic of
the suspicious nature of the people, that the same
evening, as we were dressing for dinner, the carpet
merchant begged for an interview. Our dragoman had paid for the rugs, and the merchant
suspected him of having charged me sovereigns
and paid him with Napoleons! We were able to
clear his character; he was intensely disgusted.

We had a carriage again in the afternoon.
Our drive was through a very old part of the city.

We passed out through the Salahiyeh Gate, and up a paved road. It was most wonderful that neither was our carriage upset, nor did our horses founder. But how beautiful the view was when we emerged from the village of Salahiyeh, and came to a pause on the side of a hill which towered above us on one side, while, like a magic dream, Damascus, with its green trees, and minarets, and turrets, rose out of a frame of luxuriant orchards and gardens—a vision of Paradise.

We could have remained here for hours, but we were obliged to tear ourselves away from one of the most beautiful views imaginable. We rattled down the hill in a most reckless manner, and, having arrived at the bottom without accident, went on to see a very ancient mosque on the banks of the Abana.

At the time of the Bulgarian atrocities, the persecuted Circassians fled to Turkey, which gave them various sites for villages. On our ride to Antioch we passed close to one of those. The Circassians are a very dirty people, and we saw no trace of their far-famed beauty. Having no goods of their own, their hand is against every

man, and they are much dreaded as neighbours. They have been allowed to settle round this **old** mosque, but they are worse off here than in their own country, having no apparent means of gaining a livelihood. They are bigoted Mahommedans.

We had now seen all the principal sights in Damascus, **tho** more remarkable of them I have mentioned, and our last evening in this picturesque place was come, so we told our coachman to drive us along the banks of the Abana to the gorge of the Baroda. The afternoon was **far** advanced, and the riders were prancing their horses on the green fields which grace the borders of the beautiful river. The sun was setting, and the colouring of the high cliffs above us **was** lilac; nothing could be more perfect than the lovely tints of the hills towering above the green trees which line the road. The whole air was laden with the perfume of blossoms on the shrubs growing all along the way. We took some of the branches back to the hotel, but we were obliged to put them outside our room, for the scent was too powerful.

We arrived at the gorge, and remained some

time enjoying the cool breeze and inhaling the
sweet air, quite delighted with the scene, when
we were interrupted by a request to get into our
carriage. "Quick! quick!" We obeyed, wondering
what the matter could be, for the driver
looked fearfully alarmed. We soon found out
that the dreadful diligence was approaching, and
we must fly. Our little horses went like the
wind, but nearer came the dusty monster. A
broad part of the road allowed our Jehu to gain
a place of shelter, and there we remained while
the big lumbering vehicle passed us with great
dignity, and scattered in every direction, as it
rolled on its way, the riders on horses and drivers
in carriages.

We got back to our hotel in time to dress for
the *table-d'hôte*. There was a large party at dinner,
and we were pleased to meet again the
American family whose acquaintance we had
made at Jerusalem. Among the other strangers
present were an Austrian prince and the King of
Bavaria's Master of the Horse, with his wife, a
pleasant, talkative person. As we were entering
the dining-room, an old friend I had not met for
years came up and spoke to me. The last time

I met him was at a gay ball given by my friend, Colonel Kent, and the officers of the 77th Regiment at Portsmouth. There is something very pleasant in these meetings in foreign lands, when so many "**do you** remembers" are exchanged. The old 77th **is no** more; it has vanished, and its time-honoured number has passed away; but the officers who belonged to the 77th and 88th in the old Royal Army must ever be united by a friendship formed on the battle-field, and cemented **in** many **a garrison** both at home and abroad. **The** pleasure **of** the last evening **at** Damascus was therefore increased by this meeting.

We retired early to bed, for next morning **one of** our "before dawn" starts was **to be** made. Still the dark night **was** reigning when the voice of the ever-wakeful *gurgm* was heard at **our** door proclaiming it to be half-past two **in** the morning. It is marvellous now to think how promptly **we** were astir—how, without **a** grumble, we got through tubbing and dressing, though the water of the Abana is most chilly at that hour. Then forth into the cold air we passed, guided by lanterns, to the breakfast-room, which already showed great preparations for the morning meal, **the** table being duly laid for twenty people, the most of whom had at least five hours' sleep before them. We did not linger, and soon the well-deserved backsheesh had been given, and for the last time we bowed our heads and passed through the lowly hotel wickets.

One of the hotel servants preceded us, carrying an enormous paper lantern, and we required his light, for the streets were uneven, and it was the time of intense darkness before the dawn. Behind us followed our luggage, all strapped on the back of our porter. The purchases we had made of carpets, lamps, &c., &c., had all been sent off to the diligence office the night before. We had secured the whole of the *coupé*, having felt the comfort of plenty of space and our own company on the journey up from Beyrout. We much congratulated ourselves on our forethought when we saw how many passengers were gathered round the diligence. Among them were an English lady and gentleman, who must have found it rather inconvenient where they were placed.

The drive along the banks of the Abana in the early morning was most enchanting, but the wind was cold, and we were glad to wrap ourselves in cloaks. We followed the same road we had come along from Beyrout. At the little side inn we had luncheon, and found a detachment of Turkish dragoons halted under command of a European officer who was decorated with medals, one of which was that of the Legion of Honour. The men were soldier-like in appearance, and their uniform good.

After luncheon we started again, and, as we came nearer Beyrout, a good number of passengers were taken up. At one place a nice-looking young woman in Greek costume entered the compartment in which the English lady was travelling. After a short time we heard loud exclamations, and a voice in English exclaim, "Here is a set out! This lady has been sick everywhere. How disgusting!" How matters were arranged I know not.

The view coming down the mountain upon Beyrout, looking seaward, was most beautiful. The vines were all in leaf, and all the country was green; pretty little chalets dotted the hillsides and cropped up in all sorts of impossible places. The Lebanon is well and wisely governed. The pasha lives at Beyrout. He is appointed by the Porte, and confirmed in the same by the European Powers. Theft and house-breaking are unknown, and the inhabitants of Beyrout go up to their summer resorts in the Lebanon in perfect security. As we trotted along the road, on reaching the level we met numerous carriages filled with gaily-dressed people. The horses were all greatly dismayed at the appearance of the dilly. One very well got-up phaeton and pair, with coachman and footman in livery, with cockades in their hats, nearly came to grief. The last I saw of them as we rumbled away was both nags going at full speed, and the gentleman inside the carriage evidently not at all *à son aise.*

Every Friday the pasha gives a party, and the band plays in the garden outside the town, and these were the guests whose horses we had so alarmed.

Arrived at the office in Beyrout, we found Kidby with a carriage. Our baggage delayed us some time, as it had to be passed the custom house. We drove through the town to the landing-place, where a negro employé gave us all the trouble he could with a view to being bought off, but sooner than give the man a penny he might have searched all our goods! **We** left him very much sold, with Kidby in charge to see the baggage through, and, getting into a boat, in a short time we were on board the *Griffin*, which as usual was curtseying to the Mediterranean Sea.

Next morning, the 15th of May, was Sunday. We had fulfilled **our** engagement **to be on board on** that date. The Commodore and his party had not yet arrived, but **both my** wife and myself agreed that, barring accidents, we were sure he would **turn up** on that day, for **he** never failed to fulfil any agreement of the kind. The yacht gig took **all** of us to church, including the captain, Kidby, and the two maids. It was very hot. The service was Episcopalian, which we were not prepared for, having been **in the** same church eight days ago, when the form was Presbyterian; but we had forgotten that we had been told that every alternate Sunday the service was different. One side of the aisle was completely filled by young native girls from one **of** the Christian schools; they looked pretty and modest, with their thin white veils partially covering their heads and faces.

After service, we went off to the post-office to

see if the mail-steamer that came in early had brought us letters. On our way back to the boat a man met us with the information that the Commodore and the Princess, with all their party, were on board. Poor Kidby was in a great state of distress, for he was sure "the guvner would want no end of things, and he could not get them!" The Princess's maid was equally distracted, and the captain was annoyed at being absent when the Commodore arrived. As we drew near to the yacht, the Princess appeared and waved her welcome. And when we got on deck it was like the meeting of friends who had been separated for months, instead of days. Each one had a story to relate, and we all were as jolly as possible. The Commodore informed us that he heard we were still at Damascus, and he had, with great kindness, written a note to tell us not to hurry, as he would be at Beyrout some time. This he had sent to Damascus, but it just missed us, so we never received it. Perhaps, if we had, we would have gone to see the ruins of Baalbeck. But we were quite glad to be back again, and we often said our happiness would be complete, if Kildonan and Susan were with us.

SAFED.

The twenty-two days' journeying of the Commodore and his party, from Jerusalem to Beyrout, had been a complete success. They had beautiful weather. The only place where the heat was excessive was down by the Lake of Tiberias, which was in immediate contrast with their next halting-place, Safed, where they were too cold. Safed is a very important town to the Jews, for it is there they expect the Messiah to rise from the waters of Galilee, and to take up His royal residence. Beshai, the dragoman, had done his work thoroughly well, and the cook, who came off to the yacht to say good-bye to his employers, besides being excellent in his profession, was a great wag, his face being so comical that it alone was sufficient to put one in good humour.

We had just missed at Damascus our friends, who left it the day before we arrived there, and went on to the ruined temples of Baalbeck, of whose magnificence they could not say enough, far surpassing, as they apparently did, the ruins in Egypt we had seen. From Baalbeck they went on to the cedars of Lebanon; they being only the second caravan that had got through this year, the snow had lain so late, and was so deep. However, they saw the mighty trees. It was too cold to camp up among them, so they had to ride away, carrying a number of the cones with them. The whole party looked brown and healthy after their month of tent life, but, like ourselves, though regretting their Syrian journeys were over, they were glad to be again on board the good ship *Griffin*.

On Monday some of us went to visit the Protestant colleges of Beyrout, which are on a most extensive scale, many hundreds of native girls being educated at them. Some wealthy English people have made these schools the object of their life's work, and it is impossible to say the extent of good they have done among the women of the Lebanon, where their influence must be felt in the remotest mountain and glen.

CHAPTER XIV.

GREECE RE-VISITED

PILGRIMAGE ACCOMPLISHED—VIEWS OF VARIOUS ISLANDS—THE ISLES OF GREECE—ATHENS—THE PIRÆUS—THE MASSACRE OF ENGLISH GENTLEMEN—A RUSSIAN FRIEND—TRAINS BETWEEN THE PIRÆUS AND ATHENS—ATHENIAN CABS—CHANGE IN THE ASPECT OF ATHENS—REMAINS OF ANTIQUITY—DISCOVERY OF AN ANCIENT CEMETERY—THE TOMB OF AGAMEMNON—THE EXCAVATIONS OF DR. SCHLIEMANN.

CHAPTER XIV.

AT eight in the evening on Tuesday, the 17th of May, we left the roadstead of Beyrout. Our pilgrimage in the Holy Land was over. All our adventures seemed like a dream, for my wife and I had always looked forward to the possibility of visiting Palestine, and now we had accomplished our purpose. Everything had been managed in the most agreeable way by the kindness and consideration of our Commodore and Princess, and as the darkening night obscured from view the Eastern Land it was with great regret we said farewell to its fast fading shores. The night was very fine, but the wind was from the north-west against us. When we left the anchorage at Beyrout we ceased to feel the long roll that was so trying as we lay at anchor, and which always accompanies the wind from this particular quarter.

Next day was still fine. We sighted Cyprus early, and for several hours sailed in view of that island. We made very slow progress, as during the long anchorage at Alexandria the bottom of the yacht had become covered with long grass.

The 19th of May was fine, but some thunder-showers came on, and in the evening the sky did not look quite so promising. On the morning of the 20th of May, as we sighted Scarpanto, an island near Candia, the wind increased, the thunder rolled, and the lightning flashed. At noon rain fell, and what the sailors called "coarse weather" prevailed. We were then two hundred and fifty miles from the Piræus. Every hour the weather became worse, and at night we had rain and pitch darkness, and a rough sea with contrary wind.

Next morning there was still a very rough sea. At noon we were abreast of Scarpanto, and at three in the afternoon we saw Milo a long way ahead. At night it again blew a strong gale against us, with a very heavy sea. This lasted till early on the morning of Sunday, the 22nd of

May, when the weather cleared, and the isles of Greece looked wondrous fair in the bright sunshine. The wind was cold and bracing. As the morning wore on, and we got among the islands, the sea became smooth as a mill-pond, and for the first time we saw the Mediterranean in its typical state. What a perfect sea it is, when the sun shines into its blue depths, and the only ruffle on its surface is caused by the dip of the sea-bird! A large steamer was creeping up along the shore, and picturesque boats were skimming here and there.

Mount Pentelicus, with its range of heights, rose high on the coast. And Athens next appeared in the far-off distance; and then the Piræus, with its ruins, and its new houses, and, alas! its tall chimneys, was straight in front of us. And now pilot-boats swarmed down on us; but we declined all their offers, and glided calmly on to what seemed an impossible entrance. But we were in the full light of day, which makes all the difference, going into an unknown port. Suddenly we opened up the harbour. It was crowded with men-of-war of all nations except our own. Just at the entrance we passed the tomb of Themistocles, close down at the water's edge; but my memory recalled it, as I had been in Greece many years ago.

Nothing could be gayer than the scene, as we slowly steamed up among the crowded shipping looking for a berth. Russian, French, and Greek men-of-war fly exceptionally large flags. On this occasion, which was a special one, they were enormous, the Greek royal family having gone on board the Russian flagship, in which the queen's brother is serving as a lieutenant. Besides the men-of-war, steamers from all parts were busy loading or unloading, and the shouting and vociferating and the noise of getting up steam and letting it off was incessant. We finally anchored closed to the custom house, in a very snug position, at eleven a.m. on Sunday, the 22nd of May.

The last time I was at the Piræus was as a young subaltern in the Connaught Rangers. It was marvellous to see the change these years had made in the place. The man-of-war I was in then as a guest was H.M.S. *Benbow*, commanded by the late Admiral of the Fleet, Sir Houston Stewart, G.C.B. The *Benbow* anchored off what now is a large bathing establishment. In those days the Piræus was a very small town, and the inhabitants wore the Greek costume, and swaggered about a good deal, and smoked long pipes. Now the small seaport has become a large town. The people look half French. The Greek dress is a rare sight, and the men lounge in front of the cafés smoking cigarettes. I do not think that the present stiff and modern-looking seaport is at all equal in interest or beauty to the ancient, time-worn Piræus.

We landed in the afternoon, and walked through new streets to the public gardens, where the band was expected to play. There were many little tables under the trees at which the modern Greeks quaffed tumblers of bock-bier, and presented a very different appearance from what they would have done had they been attired in their native costume. By this time a dragoman had attached himself to the Commodore, and was ready to show us all that was to be seen. We began by sitting down at one of the tables, and, having given an order for lemonade and mastique, we amused ourselves watching the people as they passed in and out among the trees. Officers in tight uniforms clattered past; nurses with children sat on benches; Greeks in ill-made coats and trousers sat in most uninteresting groups.

After a time, as the band did not appear, it was suggested that we should walk up to the height at the back of the town and have a view of Athens. Some of us shirked the climb in the heat, and only the Commodore and two ladies started. They brought back such a report of the beauty of the view, and of the easy ascent of the road, that we who had remained behind, regretted that we had done so. They had seen Athens with her glorious ruins and temples, and they saw the very spot where the unfortunate party of Englishmen had been captured by the brigands, and the dragoman had clearly pointed out the hills they had been dragged across to the fatal place where, feeling themselves hemmed in by the sea on one side and soldiers on the other, the ruffians murdered our countrymen. The feeling that was strong on our dragoman's mind, was that their guide had sold them into the hands of the brigands. He lives in Athens; but, though still professing to act as a dragoman, his trade has deserted him. The ladies said the view seaward of the thousand and one isles of Greece was enchanting, and the hilltop was covered with flowers, from which the far-famed bees of Greece were busy gathering honey. Not being of the climbing party, I returned along the quay with one of our friends, and having shouted "*Griffin* ahoy!" went on board again in the boat which was sent to take us off.

We had found out that the Russian man-of-war with whose captain we had been on such friendly terms at Algiers was lying here. The Commodore and the Princess went off to call on him, but found on arriving alongside the *Duc d'Edinbourg* that the captain had been transferred to the flag-ship, also in the harbour. So they rowed off to her, and were received with open arms by their old friend, Captain Novosilsky.

He blamed himself very much for not having found us out before we discovered him. But the ship had been *en fête* all day, owing to the Royal visitors, the King and Queen of Greece, having been on board. He came back with the Commodore, dined on board the yacht, and pathetically told us what his sorrow had been on being transferred from his own vessel to the flag-ship.

On the morning of the 23rd of May, we went on shore soon after eight o'clock, on our way to

Athens. Trains run between the Piræus and Athens every half hour. It is nothing of a journey, the distance by road being only seven miles. We had agreed that we should see more of the country going by carriage, so the dragoman had received orders to have everything ready for an early start. As we were only to be a night away from the yacht, our luggage was small, and went with us. At the landing-place we found two very superior carriages waiting for us. The Athenian cabs, as far as our experience goes, are first-rate. They are all landaus, drawn by a pair of horses, which by no means equal in excellence the carriages they draw. When I last drove along the road to Athens we were a very jolly party of officers of the *Benbow*, " some of whom are now married, and others are dead." The road is the same as it was then, only it passes through orchards; then these gardens were a bare plain. At two miles and a half from the Piræus we stopped to give the horses water, just as we had done so many years ago. The view of the Acropolis is the same as we approached nearer to the city; but a town of mean, modern houses has been built as suburbs, and the Temple of

Theseus, which was in the open when I last was here, is now almost part of a street.

Modern Athens is not interesting. As we drove on we passed through narrow streets reminding one of a French town. Shops full of modern wearing apparel were seen on both sides. If we had not known that we were in Athens we might have supposed we were in the streets of some provincial town nearer home. We dashed along Hermes Street, all new, and stopped at a grand hotel opposite the palace. We were shown to magnificent apartments *au premier*. Our rooms looked out on the palace, which is situated on a high ground, and is painfully ugly. Built of Pentelican marble, it resembles a huge manufactory. In front of it is the square, where some trees are planted. There are numbers of hotels in the Place de la Constitution.

We drove through the fashionable quarter of the town, and had pointed out to us the House of Parliament, which is not striking in any way, and the Post-Office. The streets are broad, and the houses regular. The stone of which they are built is white, and the climate does not affect the colour, which perhaps gives the impression of newness to everything.

We stopped at the museum, which is not quite finished. In it have been collected most of the treasures that, when I was in Athens last, were kept in the Temple of Theseus. The building is plain, but it is faced with the pure marble of Pentelicus, which is always beautiful. We were much struck with the extreme beauty of one of the busts in the collection. The excessive delicacy and refinement of the girl's face made us go back several times to gaze at it. There were numbers of very interesting tombstones that have been recently excavated in the vicinity of the town. In every case the deceased person is represented as seated, surrounded by a sorrowing family; one of them is invariably in the act of giving some present to the friend who is leaving them. Urns and vases of all sorts, not yet thoroughly classified, formed the bulk of the collection. There was a very perfect little figure of Minerva, which had recently been discovered.

From the museum we went to another quite modern edifice, the Academy of Arts, a very beautiful building, erected at the expense of a very wealthy Greek, who lived and died at Vienna. There are splendid lecture-rooms and libraries; floors, walls, roof, and benches, all of the whitest marble. The actual building is finished, but not the ornamental part, which is really very grand. At the entrance, under a wooden shed, a sculptor was engaged making colossal statues of Apollo and Minerva. Three gigantic figures are to be placed, at a great height, on marble pillars at the entrance to the academy.

The weather was now very hot at mid-day, so we stayed indoors during the heat of the day. In the afternoon we drove to the old ruin of Jupiter Olympus; one of its graceful pillars lies prostrate on the ground, the others are apparently firm in their place. Nothing is left of the temple but its beautifully fluted columns. We then went across the river Ilyssus, which was nearly dry, to the Amphitheatre. This has only been unearthed lately. It is a very large arena on the same principle as they were universally made in the times of the gladiators' and wild beasts' fights. We could distinctly trace the rows upon rows of seats, one above another, sufficient to accommodate thirty thousand spectators, I think, our guide said. Here once a year there is a grand renewal of the good old times. The king and queen preside, and Modern Athens pours forth its thousands to witness athletic sports and the tamer amusements of the days we live in. Our reflections on past scenes in this vast theatre were banished by the arrival of two British youths, armed with rackets, who were going to play at lawn-tennis on this classical ground. So we turned and drove away, passing again by the ruined columns of Jupiter Olympus and Hadrian's Arch on to the theatre of Dionysius.

When I was in Athens in 1842 the present beautiful marble amphitheatre was hidden by earth and rubbish, and there was nothing to be seen, as far as I remember, but the bare side of the hill, on the summit of which the Acropolis rises. But now this earth has been cleared away, and the graceful marble theatre is brought to view. We were told that what first led to excavations being made here, was the discovery of a coin, having on it a perfect representation of the theatre now unearthed. We left our carriages, and passed up among old ruins, statues, and stones, to the entrance, where a guardian admitted us. The present government most carefully look after their treasures; every temple and ruin has some one in charge. The theatre is in most wonderful preservation; the stage is as clearly marked out as in ancient days; the marble seats on which the assembled thousands sat are all in their places. The lower tier of marble seats have the names of the different owners deeply cut on them in very distinct letters. Each of the judges and statesmen, and of the great dignitaries, has his special arm-chair. This theatre was used for daylight representations. The theatre **of** Hadrian, to which we proceeded next, and which is on the same hill, was intended for night performances and competitions of music. There is every facility **for** lighting **it** up. It is on a smaller scale than the theatre of Dionysius.

From here we ascended by all that remains of the once splendid stair of seventy feet broad to the Acropolis, and entered by **the** Propylæa, a magnificent ruin of white marble. Enough of its stately columns still stands to show what it once was—it covered the whole of the western end **of** the Acropolis. The Acropolis contained all the wonderful works of art of Greece in her greatest days. Chiefest of all was the Parthenon, or Temple of Athena. This magnificent building was built on the site of a temple destroyed by the Persians four hundred and thirty-eight years B.C. Its architecture was Doric, and, like so many of the beautiful ruins of Greece, it was in purest marble. Within it stood the world-famed colossal statue of Athena, by Phidias, a master-piece of art, the unclothed parts in ivory, the drapery in plates of gold. The Parthenon remained in almost perfect preservation till A.D. 1687, when, in the siege of Athens by the Venetians, an explosion of gunpowder injured it much. The statues in the British Museum, known as the Elgin marbles, were taken from here.

The Eractheum was another very sacred building, which held the highly revered statue of Athena, formed of wood that fell from heaven, and the tombs of Erechtheus and Cecrops. On the Acropolis were many other temples and statues, principal among these, a statue of Athena Promachos in bronze, over fifty feet high. The Temple of Victory is a very perfect little building, near the entrance of the Propylæa.

The view of the surrounding country is very

fine from the corner of the walls which overlooks Athens. The mountains near Marathon are very clear, one of them having a specially sad interest now, as it is the place where our countrymen were slain by the brigands. Then, beneath us, is Modern Athens, growing larger, and encircling with its new white houses the grey old ruins **of** temples.

We remained some time enchanted with this wonderful view, yet grieving over the havoc that barbarians, rather than time, have worked. It is unfair to blame the Turk solely for the destruction of these remains of antiquity, as for years the glorious ruins have been the quarry of Greece for all their buildings.

Descending the hill to where the famous Council of Areopagus was held, we climbed its roughly-hewn steps, and stood on the spot where Paul addressed the Athenians. Here **we** can plainly see the judges' seat, and the other places where accused and accuser stood. The hill was used by the Turks as **a** burial place, and is covered with monuments. Close beside it is the Pnyx, the place of assembly for the people, almost unaltered since Paul's **time.** All this part looked little changed since the days when I last scrambled up those steps. The view from it is most interesting, as it includes the Acropolis, with its noble Parthenon, the rocks on which the prison of Socrates is situated and the Temple of Theseus, by which we drove round. The main body of this building, which is very perfect, is now used as a museum, and contains an interesting collection of sculpture, but when I was in Athens in 1842 all the *objets d'art* which have been transferred to the new museum were assembled here.

One of the most interesting of recent excavations round Athens is the discovery of an ancient cemetery. A labourer was working in his field in the suburbs of the city, when he unexpectedly came on the head of a statue. He immediately informed the authorities, and in a short time a mine of old relics was brought to light. The cemetery of olden days seems to be on exactly the same principle as that of the present time—statues and tablets with inscriptions are placed over the graves. The statues are in most perfect preservation. The groups represent a dying figure receiving from, or presenting to, the mourners standing near some remembrance. Several acres have been recovered, and no doubt the extent **of** this cemetery is very great, but the owner of the property next to the newly excavated **ground** refuses to sell his land for the sum offered, so **in** the meantime the work is stopped.

Leaving Athens from this newly-discovered City of the Dead, we had a very pleasant drive in the country to the gardens which are situated on the banks of the Ilyssus. The air was laden with the perfume of flowers, and, although the sun was hot, the road was sheltered **by** trees. We made a circuit to see **a** little of the country before stopping at Dr. Schliemann's museum, which is one of the most interesting collections I ever saw. The rich tombs of mighty Agamemnon have been rifled to supply its contents. There is an exact model to show the state in which the tomb was found. Beside the body, which lies in the centre, are placed bread and water, and in other corners the jewels and treasures that were dear to the heart of the deceased. There are several masks of thin gold, that evidently are perfect casts of the features they covered. They are all of excellent workmanship, but gave one a sad feeling that the ornaments of the great men so long dead should be exposed to view under a glass case. It is strange to gaze on these old relics, for not only are the jewels of the great dead there, but their bones and skulls and teeth.

After remaining some time in this unrivalled museum, our guide took us into the other wing of the building, which is destined as a gallery of modern pictures. As yet there are none worth looking at, but Young Greece is ambitious, and perhaps art will flourish again. We had a good view of the young queen, accompanied by her two sons, dressed in sailor costume, and by her brothers, walking from one museum to the other.

Athens was very warlike at this time, although most of the army had marched to the frontier. I saw some nice-looking recruits moving about in the streets, and there were a great number of young officers.

We endeavoured to get some antiquities to carry away from Athens, but the prices asked were so exorbitant that none of us bought anything but photographs, our stock of which was very large, as we had endeavoured to get views of all the places we visited as we went along. At

Beyrout we got very good ones of the Holy Land, but none of the photographs could be compared in clearness with those we got in Cairo.

It had been decided that we were to return to the Piræus by rail, leaving Athens at six in the evening, but we had lingered so long in **Dr.** Schliemann's museum that we could only have caught the train with a scurry; so we took matters leisurely, and went back to the hotel to settle the very heavy bill. The Commodore certainly had a fine suite of apartments, but it was a little too much to be charged for two saloons as the rooms he occupied opened out of them. On remonstrating on the price of the bed-rooms, the landlord proved he could not in fairness to himself ask less, as, if required, each room could have held another bed, so he had to charge as though it actually was there! **On** the whole, Athens was the most expensive place we visited. Rents and taxes, the people say, are so enormous that they have to make money when they get the chance.

It was a pleasant, warm evening when we drove out of Athens. We took a farewell look as we passed at the little old Byzantine church that stands in the heart of Modern Athens. Its date is of the eleventh century, and nothing can be quainter than its exterior. No one ought to go inside to be disenchanted by the tawdry hangings and painted tinsel. Another very curious little church is the old cathedral—quite a pocket affair; I do not think it would hold two dozen people. The large new cathedral rises beside it, quite dwarfing the other building. What has become of the world-renowned taste of the old Athenians? we sadly inquired, as we stood inside the edifice and looked up at the decorations made by modern Greeks.

It was nearly eight o'clock when we reached the Piræus. We drove down to the boats and pulled off to the yacht. It was always like coming home getting back to her. The captain had been doing all he could to get rid of the long grass she had acquired in Egyptian waters, but although they had scraped off cartloads, there was still enough left greatly to impede her progress. The saloons were filled with flowers, a present from our friend the Russian captain. The Commodore timed our leaving the Piræus so that next day we might have a view of the coast.

CHAPTER XV.

FAREWELL TO THE 'GRIFFIN'

DEPARTURE FROM ATHENS—NOTES OF OUR VOYAGE—STROMBOLI—STORY OF A LETTER—NAPLES AGAIN—SAIL TO ISCHIA—VIEW OF SORRENTO—A GRIM OLD EMINENCE—TERRIBLE TRAGEDY—A WEARISOME ASCENT—A PERFECTLY SITUATED HOTEL—REMINISCENCES OF AN EARTHQUAKE—A SAD STORY—BEAUTIES OF ISCHIA—MONTE NUOVO—THE COMMODORE AND PRINCESS SERENADED—TERMINATION OF OUR CRUISE—THE CZAR'S YACHT—A FEW HOURS IN NAPLES—THE AQUARIUM.

CHAPTER XV.

AT two a.m. on the morning of the 25th of May we got our anchor up and glided out between the old pier heads that guard the entrance to the harbour. A very heavy fog obscured everything, the captain told me, as I was not on deck to see it. There was a strong breeze against us, but the morning was fine when we assembled before breakfast. We were off the Gulf of Nauplia at half-past nine in the morning, abreast of the Island of Bela Poula at twelve noon, off Cape San Angelo at five in the afternoon, and rounded Cape Matapan at eleven at night. It came on to blow very hard in our teeth, with the usual accompaniment of a very rough sea. This lasted all night. The morning of the 26th of May broke gloomy, with wind and sea against us. At twelve noon we were off Navarino, and two hundred and ninety miles from the entrance of the Straits of Messina. We could only make four knots, and sometimes during the day five. The night was calm. At eight a.m., 27th of May, we were one hundred and fifty-four miles from Lighthouse Messina, and at twelve noon one hundred and twenty, so we were going seven knots. At sunset there was lightning and thunder, and on the morning of the 28th of May, as we got nearer Messina, we found a current dead against us. At eight in the morning we were in the Straits. Etna, with a sprinkling of snow on his crest, towered above us. The scenery on each side of us was very fine. Reggio, on the Italian shore, is a beautiful town, and it is much frequented in summer by the Italians. A railway runs from it to Naples, and, as steamers ply perpetually between Reggio and Messina, it makes Sicily much more accessible than in the days when the only way of reaching it was by sea from Naples. Very heavy squalls tore down upon us, and at one in the afternoon we got out of the Straits of Messina into a very heavy sea, with a gale of wind right ahead. In the evening it rained a good deal, so that we only saw Stromboli, a grim rock in the sea, but some of the sailors saw it at a later hour blazing up. Once on a passage from Sicily to Naples I had a very good view of Stromboli. The night was dark, and every now and then a great volume of flame burst forth, and the Italians on board were delighted and shouted, " Bravo, Stromboli!"

On the morning of the 29th of May we neared Capri. Rain fell, and a heavy sea saluted our entrance into the Bay of Naples, but we struggled on and anchored at five in the afternoon under a **very** grey sky, close **to** a Russian man-of-war. The *Livadia*, the Czar's most wonderful yacht, like a huge turtle with Noah's Ark on its back, rested on the water not far from us. Pratique having been procured, Kidby went on shore to get the letters, which are always a cause of great anxiety on first anchoring at any port. Sometimes they are pleasant, sometimes they are the reverse. On one occasion I remember a letter causing great consternation, and, while the Princess and her party are walking on shore, I will tell you the story of it.

My wife and I **had** been staying for some weeks in the Highlands with my sister-in-law, who had taken the manse at Abernethy. We had enjoyed our *séjour* there very much, driving and walking in the forest, and making excursions to various places of interest in that lovely neighbourhood. One afternoon, on our return from one of those pleasant drives, a man on horseback overtook us in the avenue, the bearer of a telegram for me. There was at that time no telegraph office at Abernethy, so a telegram had to be sent either by post or by messenger from Grantown, some five miles distant. As this missive had "immediate" on it, the postmistress who had charge of the telegraph-office at Grantown deemed it necessary to send it by a horseman, for which I had to pay a small fortune. The telegram was from my army agent in London, informing me that a letter had been sent to me through his office from the Horse Guards with "immediate" on it, and further stating that the postmistress at Grantown had been requested to forward the letter as soon as it arrived. This request may appear superfluous, as letters are usually delivered when received; but there are exceptions to the rule in the Highlands, where posts arrive perhaps twice a week, and letters are delivered through a sparsely populated district by a carrier walking twenty miles a day. Sometimes the post becomes *poste restante*.

But Grantown is a large place on the Highland railway, with its daily post. Now the postmistress had sent the telegram, but not the letter. There was nothing for it but to wait till next day, when the usual post would certainly bring 'the missing letter.

Next day came, **but** not the official missive. I then hired a man and horse to go into Grantown to bring the missing document, for which I gave him five shillings. The man returned with **a** message from the postmistress that no letter had yet arrived, but, as soon as it did come, it would be sent off to Abernethy. My wife and I were much annoyed **at** all these complications. Both of us felt convinced that an appointment at length had come, and that the offer of a command of **a** division either at home or abroad was what was contained in the letter, for why should the Horse Guards write "immediate" on the envelope? That evening was passed in speculating about where the division would be. If in India, would I accept it? We left the decision **an** open question. Next morning the post arrived, but still no letter. This really was becoming very trying. My sister-in-law promised that after luncheon she would drive us into Grantown to the post-office. It is a pleasant drive; but I saw none of its beauties, nor did my wife. Our thoughts were too much occupied. I sat up on the box near the coachman, so as not to have to talk. I made up my mind to take an English horse as charger out to India, and arranged many details in my mind. I feel certain my wife had been equally busy with our future. We drove into Grantown, and found a mild and rather frightened-looking woman at the counter of the shop in which was the post-office. In hurried accents I asked for the letter marked "Immediate."

"Oh, sir, that letter I sent to Abernethy."

"Impossible!" I exclaimed, "we have just driven from there."

"Ah! but, sir," replied the alarmed post-mistress, "the laddie that took it will have gaun the short road to the manse; ye'll have missed him. I'm vera sorry!"

"Boof!" I fear was my answer. Now this was really becoming beyond a joke. It was like a bad **dream**. We must return **to** Abernethy again. So **we** retraced our steps. By the time we got there I had composed in my mind many letters to friends, tradesmen, and horse-dealers. How delightful it was to think of being once more in harness, and what a pleasure it would be to have my old friend Moore as my A D C, if he would accept the office!

The approach to the manse at Abernethy is very long, and up a hill. I thought the horses would never arrive. **At** length the door was reached. **I** jumped off the box, and was quickly followed by the others into the drawing-room. The letter was there on the table. How well I see the whole scene now! My sister-in-law took up a newspaper and pretended to read; my wife's colour rapidly changed from red to white. I know my hand shook. But it must be done, so I opened the envelope, and took out the officially-folded paper, which informed me in the usual language that it had been decided that general officers, having attained the age of seventy, were to be placed on a retired list, and requesting me to inform the War Office of the date of my birth, if recollected.

Early next morning we left Naples on our last expedition in the *Griffin*. The beautiful bay was at its brightest and best. Vesuvius was clearly defined against the blue sky, and volumes of smoke came from its summit. We were bound for Ischia. The Commodore had passed many weeks in the island a few years ago, and so had the Princess, and Ischia was full of reminiscences for them. We steamed quietly away. The *Griffin* seemed to enjoy the rare luxury of a calm sea after all the troubles she had gone through. Sorrento and the coast along the bay were lovely to look at, and as we came nearer to Ischia the high hills, so green and fertile, rose like enchantment above the calm, blue sea. The Commodore pointed out to us a grim old building on a height, in the interior of which, while he was living on the island, some alterations were being made. While these were proceeding, the workmen came upon a walled-up cell, containing the remains of some unhappy women, but what their crime had been can never now be known. All that could now be seen was that they had been shut up with food and water. The workmen hastily built up the wall again, so that their prison still continues to be their **tomb**. We anchored outside the little port, and several boats came off, one of them owned by an old acquaintance of the Commodore, who seemed overjoyed to meet him again.

We all went **on** shore. The advent of the yacht in the bay had brought every carriage in the place to the landing, also donkeys and horses, **all** in hopes of obtaining a fare. Had I known one quarter of the length of the hill we had **to** climb, they should **have** found a ready customer in me, but I imagined it was only **a** step, and leisurely followed the rest of the party, generally arriving at a turn in the road to see them disappearing round another turn considerably in advance, and always, as I fondly hoped, **the** last. The road was between high walls or steep banks, and it was oppressively hot. **A** boy attached himself to me, who spoke English, and gave me various details of the earthquake that had wrought such havoc in this fair island only a few months before. But the hill was getting steeper, and we seemed no nearer our journey's end; the boy said farewell as soon as his house was reached, but before he left me I inquired, "Where are we going to?" He pointed up to the clouds and disappeared. Excelsior!

At last, turning aside into a long alley of orange-trees, commanding such a view of sea and land that no painter or poet could do justice to it, we found ourselves in the most perfectly situated hotel, so full of reminiscence to some of our number. We were most warmly welcomed by the handsome Italian landlady, and on both sides there were inquiries after the health and welfare of old friends.

The fearful earthquake was the one topic of conversation in Ischia. In this house, where, comparatively speaking, it had done little harm, many of the walls were split, costly mirrors had been shattered, but here no lives had been lost. The poor landlady could hardly mention the subject without agitation, but, like many people whose nerves have been shattered by some dreadful event, could not help speaking on the subject. Her dilated eyes looked as though they still saw the horrors that were so visibly present to her remembrance. She and her family were at their midday meal, when, without previous warning, the shock came. The wave of earthquake in its full force rolled down the ravine in which the town is situated. The hotel, which is some distance off, only felt the swell of the wave, which was sufficient to shake the house to its very foundations, as we saw. But it was in the town itself that its terrible force was felt. The houses toppled over like a pack of cards, burying living and dead in their ruins; and, when the first dreadful panic passed, then could be heard the cries of those that were engulfed in the ruins, beseeching release. The news was telegraphed at once to Naples, and in a few hours a strong body of military were on the spot, who began to work at disinterring the living. Our landlady's brother had two children buried alive. He was like a madman, she said, as he listened to the cries, and yet powerless to save his little ones; for at six o'clock in the evening the bugle sounded "Cease work," and, leaving pickaxe and spade for food and rest, the soldiery left the entombed victims for another twelve hours. And so the days wore on, and no living were rescued. It was a dreadful story to listen to, and we looked with sorrowful compassion at the haggard, worn man who had gone through such a fearful trial.

Our luncheon was sumptuous, and the country wines were excellent. The worthy landlady would not hear of receiving payment; the pleasure was hers, she said, entertaining her old friends.

We proceeded to visit the ruins of the town. We passed along a smiling road, with foliage clustering on trellised wooden palings. All nature seemed asleep in the glowing warmth of the sun. It was a kind of earthly Paradise. Too earthly, alas!—for, as we entered the street of the town, a ruined house met our astonished gaze; not one, but every habitation was roofless and crumbling to the ground. The whole place reminded me of a town which had been destroyed by bombardment. But that takes time; all this havoc had been effected in one moment. Not one single dwelling was inhabitable, although some of the poor owners still fondly clung to their once happy homes. We came to the principal church. The clock had stopped at the hour, twenty minutes to one, I think. The building was rent from top to bottom, and the large crucifix on the altar had been turned completely round. All this misery and death came on the inhabitants of the town in one moment.

Our guide showed us a wine-shop where two men were playing at draughts, both of whom were killed by the falling walls. **At** another house one man was writing in an inner room, and another was standing at the door; the writer was killed, the other escaped with his life. **An** old **man** was leading a child by the hand; the old man was killed, the child was saved.

The morning had been dark and heavy with clouds, but all was very still. The people were busy in their various occupations. Some were at their dinners, others playing games, and many strolling about. A sudden shock, a united scream of hundreds of voices, and the town crumbled away and swallowed up young and old in one fearful catastrophe. And those who had escaped made a good trade by their misfortunes. If they ever had any diffidence in begging, they have none now. Women, who perhaps were modest, happy mothers of families, have become bold and importunate beggars—it was a sad and woeful sight. As we emerged from the ruins we found two carriages, that had persistently followed us all the morning, still waiting in the confident hope that we should not be able to resist driving at last— nor did we disappoint them.

The zigzagging road down the hill to the sea is perfectly lovely, every turn disclosing fresh beauty. High above us towered Mount San Nicolo, an extinct volcano of irregular shape; it rises about two thousand six hundred feet above the level of the sea. The whole island is evidently of volcanic origin; the shape of its mountains, the deep chasm and fissure in the hill-sides, and the constant presence of lava all point to it. The surface is wonderfully fertile, and every fruit-tree seems to have its home in the island. During the hot months of summer visitors swarm into Ischia, but we were too early to see anything of the season. We embarked again in the yacht's gig, and, on nearing the *Griffin*, found a large boat full of "musicianers," who had come off to serenade the Commodore and the Princess in memory of old times. Largesse having been distributed with a liberal hand, if one could judge from the smiles of the recipients, we "hove anchor" again, and proceeded to steam round the

Island of Ischia on our homeward cruise. Very high cliffs frown down on the bold and presumptuous waves, which leap and tumble in the perpetual attempt to ascend these rugged rocks. As we rounded the island, and made towards Naples, the sky became dark and lowering, and the white houses on the mainland stood out bright and clear.

Vesuvius sent out much black smoke, and although the sea was calm, yet it seemed to **portend** evil, but the white-sailed vessels pursued their voyage unheeding, and the thunder showers poured down on the coast to leeward. It was a fine sight, but not what we hoped for in these sunny climes,—storm and rain, instead **of** light breezes and calm sea. As we came near **our** anchorage in the harbour of Naples, it was with much regret that I called to mind it was the last time that we should hear the captain's hail of "let go!" **Our** voyage had come to a close, and soon the family on board the *Griffin* would cease to exist as a whole.

We anchored in a better position than the one we had first taken up. When night came **on** Vesuvius sent forth red flames which licked the air, accompanied with black volumes of smoke.

Admiral Popoff, who had called on the Commodore, was on board the *Livadia*, that huge, ugly floating monster, the Czar's yacht. I should like to have gone on board of her, but neither my wife nor I could join the Princess's party, as we had to make arrangements for our departure from Naples. So, when the Commodore proceeded to the *Livadia*, we landed at the Custom House, and, having got a carriage, drove off to find out about trains, etc. We were anxious to be in Paris by Sunday, the 5th of June. It was a long journey to take without stopping, but we proposed breaking it by sleeping at Turin. We found that our best route was by Rome and Genoa to Turin, and then by the Mont Cenis tunnel to Paris. With considerable satisfaction, we discovered that, if we left Naples next morning by an early train, we should be in Turin within twenty-four hours, which would leave us a day and a night to rest, and twenty more hours would take us to Paris on Saturday morning.

As the forenoon was still young, we told our coachman to take us up the Strada Emanuele to have a look once again at the beautiful bay and the treacherous sea that we were so soon to leave. An immense deal has been done to improve Naples since I was last here, six years ago, and one of the greatest improvements is in the hired cabs, the horses of which used to be most miserable animals, and were treated with great cruelty with their fearful nose-bits. Now they are well groomed and in good condition. Doubtless the Society for the Prevention of Cruelty to Animals has effected this. Formerly, when **in** Naples, **I** never went out without seeing some case of hideous cruelty, but now in the few hours I was there I saw none. The mania for building has extended to the south, for everywhere **at** Naples new streets were springing **up.**

We returned on board to find the Commodore's party just come back from their visit to the *Livadia*. They had been received with the greatest courtesy by the Admiral, and had been shown over the whole of the wonderful monster. The luxury of her arrangements amazed all who beheld them—they said she was not like a **ship,** as there was nothing to remind them of the sea— she was a floating palace. The naval officers were very comfortably put up, which is far from being the case in some other Russian men-of-war. The Admiral vowed that, during the worst weather he had been out in the *Livadia*, the most she had rolled was four degrees! He designed her,—so let us congratulate him on his success.

After luncheon we all went on shore except my wife, who insisted that packing must be done. We drove first to the Aquarium, where we had to pay two francs each for tickets of admission, which at first seemed a good deal, but the price was not too much for such a valuable exhibition.

I never saw a more interesting collection, and the care which was taken of everything was most creditable. One very curious sight was that of the coral actually in the course of construction by the tiny coral insects. In one section, sea-horses swam past, and I saw a cockle make a bound in the water and come gently down again, to my great surprise, as I always thought they were most sedentary in their habits! The guardian, seeing how interested we were, took great pains to show off his sea treasures—poking into sand and bringing to the surface fish which lie perdu on the sea-shore in the sand and only leave a point exposed, on which the fishermen sometimes tread and are severely wounded. From the Aquarium we drove up the hill above Naples and got another view as lovely as that of the morning.

Heavy black smoke came from Vesuvius and we heard afterwards that an eruption had taken place on the night of the 1st of June, the day we left Naples.

After the charming drive we returned on board to dinner. Our comfortable cabins now looked dismantled; everything was packed. How much I regretted that the last night on board had come!

It is a strange thought that everything comes to an end. Six months ago we were looking forward to this cruise, and **now** it was over. How many places we had seen—how many perils had **we** encountered—how much kindness **had we** received! All was over now.

Very early next morning we were on deck. Our always kind and courteous hosts were up to see us off. Their cruise was to be prolonged for a few days as far as Marseilles.

The first intention had been to put the *Griffin* in dock at Naples and have her cleaned, but a man-of-war was already on the slip, and would be there for another three weeks. She was ultimately dry-docked at Marseilles, and had a splendid quick passage home.

It was with much regret that final farewells were said. The gig took us three on shore, Parker having to be in London on the 4th of June, and when we shook hands with the boat's crew, having parted with Captain Oman and all our other sailor friends on board, and took a last look at the yacht, we felt very sad that never again should we be called on to shout

"GRIFFIN AHOY!"

THE END.

LONDON : PRINTED BY DUNCAN MACDONALD, BLENHEIM HOUSE.

www.ingramcontent.com/pod-product-compliance
Lightning Source LLC
Chambersburg PA
CBHW031855220426
43663CB00006B/640